لقد كان عبرة لأولى

*erstanding…"* — SURAH YUSUF, VERSE 111

ANOTHER OUTSTANDING PRODUCTION

معمد غفور الدين

بِسْمِ اللهِ الرَّحْمَنِ الرَّحِيمِ

In the name of Allah, the most Merciful, most Kind

## Abul Noor
### PUBLICATIONS

ISBN: 978-0-9571096-5-0

Title: **True Stories of Islam Volume II**
Author: **Sultanul Wa'izeen Maulana Abul Noor Muhammad Bashir**
Translator: **Shahid Hussain**

Published by **Abul Noor Publications,**
Leicester, United Kingdom

Website: **www.abulnoor.com**
Email: **publications@abulnoor.com**

Cover design by Zain ul-Abedin (Faadil)

Calligraphy by Ibne Kaleem Ahsan Nizami

## OUTSTANDING

Designed, printed & bound in the
United Kingdom by OUTSTANDING
Email: books@standoutnow.co.uk
Tel: +44 (0)121 327 3277

# TRUE
# STORIES
## OF
# ISLAM

## VOLUME II

WRITTEN BY

SULTAN-UL-WAIZEEN

MAULANA ABUL NOOR

MUHAMMAD BASHIR

TRANSLATED BY

SHAHID HUSSAIN

Abul Noor
PUBLICATIONS

# Contents

## PART SIX

### THE AHL AL-BAYT

### (MAY ALLAH BE PLEASED WITH THEM ALL)

## PART SEVEN

### THE FOUR IMAMS OF FIQH
### (MAY ALLAH BE PLEASED WITH THEM ALL)

# Foreword to volume II

الحمد لله رب العالمين و العاقبة للمتقين و الصلاة
و السلام علي سيد الأنبياء و المرسلين

Four years on from the publication of True Stories of Islam Volume I, I am delighted and honoured to present to you True Stories of Islam Volume II, which is the continuation of the authorised translations of 'Sachhi Hikayaat' the work of the honourable Sultanul Wa'izeen Mawlana Abul Noor Muhammad Bashir (may Allah have mercy upon him, Ameen).

True Stories of Islam Volume I, by the grace and favour of Allah, was positively received by those who read it and I received numerous words of congratulations and encouragement for undertaking this work. The thing that pleased me most with the first volume was that it was quickly adapted by many Islamic Schools (Madrassas) throughout the United Kingdom. I was often asked, 'when is True Stories Volume II coming out?' Alhamdulillah, the wait is over and it delights me to be able to present this book.

This book is split neatly into two parts:

- The Ahl al-Bayt – the House of the Prophet ﷺ
- The Imams and founders of the Four Madhhabs.

Like before, all stories are referenced and each story has a short summary or 'moral', which aims to highlight the main points. Written in clear and simple English, this book will be ideal for Muslims of all ages, from young Madrassa students to older readers.

The key feature of the book is a detailed account on the life and martyrdom of Sayyiduna Imam al-Husayn﷜. The Karbala story is a poignant one and the lessons of it are important not just for Muslims, but for all of humanity.

There are many people deserved of mention in regards to this latest publication. First and foremost I want to mention my honourable brother Dr Hafiz Ather Hussain al-Azhari, who has supported me again throughout the project and was very helpful in proofreading and providing advice. I would also like to thank Maulana Salim Patel Noorie of Canada for his invaluable time in proofreading the manuscript. My deepest gratitude and appreciation goes to Zain al-Abedin Hussein of Outstanding for putting this book together in such a beautiful format and for putting up with me with all the incessant but necessary amendments in the final stages of this project. Last and by no means least, I want to give special mention and thanks to the inspiration for this translation, and that is the son of Sultanul Wa'izeen, Sahibzada Allama Ata al-Mustafa Jameel (may Allah preserve him and grant him a long life, Ameen).

Loving the Prophet'sﷺ family is a fundamental duty that cannot be neglected - this book intends to infuse that love for them by shedding light on their illustrious and noble lives. With these thoughts it leaves me to conclude by saying thank you for purchasing this book. I sincerely pray that this translation is a means of my salvation in the hereafter and that it brings to the reader real love for the noble characters mentioned, Ameen.

**Shahid Hussain**

Leicester
August 2020 / Dhu'l Hijjah 1441

I have five by which I extinguish the destructive fire/plague

Al Mustafa 🌼, Al Murtada 🌼, their two sons and Fatima 🌼

# PART SIX

## THE AHL AL-BAYT

## (MAY ALLAH BE PLEASED WITH THEM ALL)

إِنَّمَا يُرِيدُ اللَّهُ لِيُذْهِبَ عَنكُمُ الرِّجْسَ أَهْلَ الْبَيْتِ وَيُطَهِّرَكُمْ تَطْهِيرًا

Allah only desires O members of the family of the Prophet!
That He may remove from you all uncleanliness and
purify you well after cleaning you thoroughly...

(33:33)

# Mother of the believers
## Sayyida Khadija ﷺ

Khuwaylid was a rich man of the Quraysh tribe. He had a daughter named Khadija. She was a beautiful and intelligent lady who was among the most respected women in Makkah at the time. Khuwaylid left the world a rich man leaving all his wealth to his only daughter. She had a cousin named Waraqa ibn Nawfal who she could now rely on but she took the job of maintaining her late father's business herself. Abu Talib, uncle to the Prophet ﷺ, got his nephew to work for Khadija's trading business. After working a short while for her, she noticed a significant increase in her business.

One day, Khadija was standing on the rooftop on a hot day when she saw the final Prophet ﷺ walking by. What she saw was a cloud protecting him as he walked along. The cloud followed the Prophet ﷺ wherever he went. She was intrigued by what she saw and it made her more curious about him. One day she called the Prophet ﷺ and told him that she wished that he would go on her trade convoy to Syria. The Prophet ﷺ agreed. Khadija called upon Maysarah her servant and told him that the Prophet ﷺ would join them. He was told that they should do whatever he said and to copy whatever he did. He was also told to note his every action throughout the journey. Maysarah heard all what Khadija had to say and agreed to follow her commands. A few days later the convoy left for Syria, which included the Prophet ﷺ. On the way there they stopped by a Christian monastery to take a little rest. This was the place of a monk named Nastur. Prophet Muhammad ﷺ sat down under the shade of the tree as the monk met Maysarah. The monk instantly took note of the man under the tree and asked Maysarah who the man was. The servant replied that this man is a respected man of the Quraysh tribe and that he was their leader. The monk said he is not only your leader for this convoy but for the entire world! Maysarah was interested in what the monk had to say and asked him how he knew that? The monk replied that he could tell from his eyes. 'There is no one other than a Prophet sitting in the shade of that tree. I know he is the last Prophet. Only if I could live to see his prophethood'! The monk told Maysarah not to part from him and told him to behave well with him because Allah has made him His final Prophet.

The eventful journey ended as the convoy reached its destination. With the blessings of the Prophet ﷺ Khadija's goods were sold in Syria earning them a good profit. The convoy were delighted at the business transaction as they headed back towards Makkah. All the convoy members were ecstatic at the effort of Muhammad in their business transaction. As they approached Makkah it became the wish of its members that Muhammad should be the first one to tell Khadija about the good news. He agreed and rode off ahead of the convoy to tell Khadija the good news. The Prophet was entering Makkah when at that time Khadija was on her rooftop. She saw an enlightened man riding a horse with a cloud following the rider. The sight of him on his horse riding majestically with a cloud over him again intrigued Khadija. The Prophet ﷺ arrived at her house and told her the good news that her goods were sold successfully in Syria. Soon after the rest of the convoy led by Maysarah reached Makkah to share in the celebrations. Maysarah told Khadija about everything that had happened including the incident with the monk under the tree. Khadija after hearing all this became utterly convinced that he was no ordinary person but a very special man indeed. Khadija waited for a few days and then approached the Prophet ﷺ for his hand in marriage. The Prophet ﷺ told her that his uncle Abu Talib would need to be consulted on the matter. Khadija went to Abu Talib and told him about her proposal to his nephew. Abu Talib was worried about the age difference between the couple but after talking to his wife agreed to the marriage. Waraqa ibn Nawfal, Abu Talib, Hamza and other friends and family gathered for the marriage ceremony. After the ceremony Khadija announced that all her wealth, business assets and so forth were now in the hands of the Prophet ﷺ, her husband. She gave him permission to spend the money as he saw fit. When the Prophet ﷺ announced his prophethood, the wealth of Khadija came to his aid in times of need. Khadija spent the rest of her life in looking after and serving our beloved Master ﷺ.

*al Mawahib al-Laduniyya, Tarikh Islam*

---

*The Mother of the Believers* Sayyida Khadija ؓ was the first wife of Sayyiduna Muhammad ﷺ. She lived an exemplary life, which showed virtues that were generally lacking amongst women at the time. Her generosity knew no bounds and gave everything in the way of Allah and His Messenger. The Prophet was twenty-five years old and Khadija was forty years old when they married. He married no one else while Khadija was still in his life. It was only after her death that he married again. This shows the love, honour, respect and esteem our Prophet ﷺ had for her. By marrying Khadija, the Prophet ﷺ initiated a Sunnah, which he desires for his Ummah. The Prophet ﷺ came as a moral guide to living life. Khadija bore all of the Prophet's children except Ibrahim ؓ whose mother was Sayyida Mariya ؓ. Her four daughters were Sayyida Zaynab, Sayyida Ruqayya, Sayyida Umm Khulthum and Sayyida Fatima Zahrā ؓ. The scholars of Islam are of the consensus that the Prophet ﷺ had four daughters from Khadija ؓ.

• 265 •

# Mother of the believers Sayyida Aisha ؓ

After the death of Sayyida Khadija, the Prophet married Sayyida Aisha, the daughter of Abu Bakr. The Messenger of Allah ﷺ once told Aisha that before their marriage, he had a dream three nights in a row in which an angel showed her in a beautiful green suit. The angel told him that this lady would become his wife in this world and in the hereafter. Sayyiduna Jibreel ؑ also appeared once and showed her in another beautiful garment. He gave the good news that he will marry her and will remain together forever.

*Mishkat Sharif, Al-Mawahib al-Laduniyya*

*The Mother of the Believers*, Sayyida Aisha has a great status. She is the beloved of the Holy Prophet in this world and in the hereafter. Their marriage was divinely ordained. So therefore any remarks against her personality and her qualities undoubtedly would cause him hurt and anguish and ultimately they question the will and wisdom of Allah's plans.

# A great allegation

It was in the fifth year after Hijra, that the Battle of Banu al-Mustaliq took place. The Prophet of Allah was returning from this battle when the following incident took place. The convoy was approaching al-Madina when it stopped for a break. Sayyida Aisha got off her camel to go and relieve herself. She somehow lost her necklace and began looking for it. The convoy thought that Aisha had returned and set off again. Aisha returned to see that the convoy had left without her. She was anticipating the convoy to realise their mistake and to return. As she waited she covered herself with her shawl. In those days it was the custom of the Arabs to appoint someone who stays behind at every stopping point of a journey to see if anything was left behind. On this occasion this responsibility was left to Safwan. He went about his task when he discovered Aisha. He thought she had passed away and said "from Allah, we come and to Him is our return'. Safwan lifted Aisha and placed her on his camel and took her back to al-Madina to tell them what he thought was the bad news. As they reached al-Madina, Safwan realised that she was not dead. The hypocrites in al-Madina saw this as an opportunity to spread dissent and mischief. They began to make allegations that Safwan did something to Aisha (Ma'azallah- God Forbid). Aisha heard of these allegations and made her feel sick. She was ill for a month. During this time she had little idea of what sort of absurdities the hypocrites were uttering. She would not stop crying during this time and nor could she sleep. The Prophet 🌼 was sent a revelation in which Allah affirmed the purity and chastity of the Prophet's beloved wife. All those people who spread lies and allegations about Aisha and whoever listened to them and accepted them were all punished.

> **...For each man among them is sin that he has earned;**
> **and for the one among them who played the greatest**
> **part in it for him is a terrible punishment .**
>
> (24:11)

*Qur'an Surah Nur, Khazahinul Irfan*

Sayyida Aisha's chastity and purity has been mentioned and clarified in the Holy Qur'an and for eternity this will remain so. Furthermore the punishment for those that spread the false allegations upon her has also been made abundantly clear. So those that persist in questioning about her honour and status are surely inviting the wrath of Allah for ignoring the Qu'ran's decisive verdict on the matter.

• 267 •

# Witnesses

As the hypocrites continued to whip up a frenzy of false allegations and rumours against Sayyida Aisha, the Prophet took to his pulpit and addressed his noble Companions. 'O Muslims! Who from among you will defend the honour against the attacker of the person who has transgressed all bounds in doing harm to me by slandering my wife?'

Sayyiduna Umar﷜ responded and said: 'The hypocrites are undoubtedly false and the *Mother of the Believers* is undoubtedly pure and chaste. Allah does not allow flies to sit on you because they sit on filth. Is He the Almighty not going to safeguard you from filthy women?'

Sayyiduna Uthman﷜ rose and said similar words and added 'Allah does not allow your shadow to fall on the ground so that it is not stepped on. How is it possible that the Lord of all the worlds who protects your shadow would not protect your family?'

Sayyiduna Mawla Ali﷜ rose and said 'Allah instructed you to remove your blessed sandals because there was some flies blood on it. How would the Lord who could not tolerate that tiny amount of impurity on your sandals tolerate any impurity in your family?'

Several other noble Companions spoke and reiterated the message that Sayyida Aisha﷜ was undoubtedly pure and chaste and the hypocrites words were false. The Holy Prophet took immense comfort in the action and words of his Companions who totally disregarded the whispers and rumours. Sayyida Aisha﷜ learnt of this assembly and was comforted by the unanimous belief of the noble Companions.

*Khazahinul Irfan, Ruhul Bayan, Madarij al-Nabuwwa*

---

To speak ill of the Ahl al-Bayt is the way of the hypocrites, not the believers. We should therefore follow the footsteps of the noble Companions and avoid the path of the deviated and misguided. The Prophet of Allah had full knowledge and certainty that his beloved wife Aisha﷜ did nothing wrong. Indeed he said 'I swear to Allah I know my wife is good'. But the Prophetﷺ being the judge cannot testify for himself but needs witnesses to do that. In a normal case, the judge has to decide on the evidence of the witnesses. This is exactly what the Prophetﷺ did by calling upon his Companions for 'character references' of Sayyida Aisha﷜. Similarly Allah Almighty, on the Day of Judgement will know very well each and every individual case that is brought before Him. But Allah will call upon a witness who will give evidence for everyone from Adam﷜ to the 'last man'. And that witness is no other than the final Prophet Muhammadﷺ. If the Prophet of Allah had decided for himself without witnesses, which would have sufficed, then the verse in Surah Nur would not have been revealed and recited by believers until the Day of Judgement.

# Husband's love

One day Sayyiduna Muhammadﷺ said to his beloved wife Aishaﷺ "O Aishaﷺ! When you are happy I know it, and when you are sad I also know it." Aishaﷺ heard this and asked "O Messenger of Allah! 'How do you know?" The Prophet replied, "When you are happy, you say 'I swear by the Lord of Muhammadﷺ! But when you are not happy you say 'I swear by the Lord of Ibrahim!" (The Prophet's son who died in infancy). Aishaﷺ said "O Prophet! This is true but my love for you is the same and will never change."

*Madarij al- Nabuwwa*

Every action and saying of our dear Prophetﷺ is a valuable lesson to us all. We learn from this story that a husband or wife should not stop loving each other.

# Generosity

*The Mother of the Belivers* Sayyida Aishaﷺ was an extremely generous woman. Urwa ibn Zubayr says that in one day she spent seventy thousand Dirhams in the way of Allah. Abdullah ibn Zubayr once gave Sayyida Aishaﷺ one hundred thousand Dirhams. She spent all that money in the way of Allah on that day. She also happened to be fasting. When it came to break the fast, the helper for Sayyida Aishaﷺ told her that there was no food. 'Had you saved a Dirham we could have ordered meat and ate that?' Aisha replied: 'I forgot, otherwise we could have brought some meat'.

*Madarij al-Nabuwwa*

---

Sayyida Aisha ﷞ lived a very simple life in accordance to the Sunnah of the Prophet ﷺ. Any wealth she did get would be spent in the way of Allah feeding the poor and so on. We should follow the way of Aisha ﷞ and not indulge in expensive luxuries that distract us from remembering and fearing Allah.

• 270 •

# Auntie

Sayyida Aisha ﷞ loved her nephew Abdullah ibn Zubayr very much that she took care of him. Abdullah ibn Zubayr would see on a regular occurrence his aunt spend any money she had in charity. One day he said "O Aunt! You should stop your hand." Aisha understood by what her nephew meant and became angry with this. She then vowed not to talk to him again until he had apologised. Abdullah ibn Zubayr began to feel the effects of his Auntie's silent protest and began to ask people to help him resolve the issue. Abdullah became very anxious of the situation that he called upon two members of Aisha's household to help him. The two 'negotiators' entered Aisha's house and began talking. Abdullah followed them in and hid. No sooner did they start talking Abdullah fell at the feet of his aunt and began crying and sought her forgiveness. The two 'negotiators' also pleaded with Aisha to forgive him. They told her by stating a Hadith of the Holy Prophet ﷺ about the dangers of imposing a no talk policy on relatives and Muslims. She began to cry. She forgave Abdullah ibn Zubayr and began talking with him again. For expiating her oath she freed twelve slaves at a time. And from then on whenever the thought of breaking a promise came to her mind she would weep in fear of Allah so much that her headscarf would get drenched in tears.

*Sahih al-Bukhari, Hikaya al-Sahaba*

---

The people of Allah only became angry or disappointed in matters that pertain to religion and not worldly matters. We learn that the sayings of the Prophet 🌺 cool down the hearts and minds of people. We also learn that any oath taken in the name of Allah must be carried out. And if for any reason it is broken then it should be expiated for appropriately. Fear of Allah is a state of a person who regrets their mistakes and if they even think about it again start to cry in fear that they may commit it again.

• 271 •

# Blessed Chamber

When Sayyiduna Muhammad 🌺 left this mortal world, he was buried in the room of Sayyida Aisha 🌺. *The Mother of the Believers* would regularly go and visit the Prophet's grave by sending her salaams and by telling the Prophet about her feelings. She entered the room as she pleased because her husband was buried there and because it was her room. When her father, the first Caliph, Sayyiduna Abu Bakr Siddiq 🌺 passed away, he was buried next to the Prophet 🌺 as he requested. She would enter the room often and send her salaams to her blessed husband and father. But when Sayyiduna Umar Faruq 🌺 passed away and was buried in the Blessed Chamber, Sayyida Aisha 🌺 would take great care and respect when entering her room. There was now a non-Mahram present so she would cover herself properly. Whenever she went in from that day on, she felt it necessary to possess more modesty than usual because a non-Mahram was now present.

*Mishkat Sharif*

The dead (Muslim and non-Muslim alike) can see, hear and recognise those who attend their grave. Sayyida Aisha۝ had the belief that the Prophet۝ and his two close Companions are alive in their graves.

• 272 •

# *Mother of the believers* Sayyida Hafsa۝

The daughter of Sayyiduna Umar۝ Sayyida Hafsa was married to Khunays. But he soon died leaving Hafsa widowed. Sayyiduna Uthman۝ lost his wife Ruqayyah. Umar approached Uthman offering his daughter's hand in marriage to him. Uthman kept silent on the issue and gave no indication of his intentions. Umar۝ was somewhat frustrated by this response and went to the Prophet۝. The Prophet۝ heard what Umar had to say and said "Shall I not tell you of a better person to take your daughter's hand in marriage?" The Prophet۝ took Hafsa's hand in marriage. And Uthman was given the Prophet's other daughter Umm Khulthum in marriage.

*Madarij al-Nabuwwa*

The four Caliphs of Islam have a spiritual and blood relationship with our Prophet۝. Sayyiduna Abu Bakr and Umar۝ became the father-in-laws of the Prophet, while Sayyiduna Uthman and Ali۝ are his sons-in-law.

## *Mother of the believers*
## Sayyida Zaynab bint Jahsh ﷺ

Zayd ibn Haritha was dearly loved by the Prophet of Allah ﷺ and he took him as his adopted son (Mutabanni). He arranged for his marriage to take place with Zaynab bint Jahsh. They did so but the marriage was an unhappy one and they agreed to divorce after about a year together.

Sometime later the Prophet of Allah ﷺ married her and made her one of the *Mother of the Believers*. The hypocrites residing in al-Madina began to say amongst themselves say that 'The Prophet has married his daughter in Law.' (God forbid).

Allah sent revelation and refuted the thoughts of the hypocrites.

**And it is not befitting to a Muslim man or Muslim woman, when Allah and His Messenger have decreed something that they would have any choice in their matters, and whoever disobeys Allah and His Messenger, he undoubtedly, has strayed away manifestly.**

**And O beloved! Remember when you did say to him whom Allah bestowed a favour and you had bestowed a favour, 'keep your wife with yourself and fear Allah and you had in your heart what Allah had willed to disclose and you were afraid of people's taunting remarks; and Allah has a greater right that you should fear Him. Then when Zaid had accomplished his purpose with her, We gave her in your marriage, so that there should be no hindrance upon the Muslims in respect of the wives of their adopted sons when they have accomplished their purpose with them. And Allah's order is bound to be fulfilled.**

There is no hindrance for the Prophet regarding that which Allah has appointed for him. Such has been the practice of Allah among those who have gone before and the command of Allah is the ordained destiny.

Those who deliver the messages of Allah, fear Him, and fear none except Allah. And Allah is Sufficient as a Reckoner. Muhammad is not the father of any of your men; yes He is the Messenger of Allah and the last one among all the prophets. And Allah knows all things.

(33:36-40)

When she learnt of the revelation she fell in to prostration in thanks to Allah that her marriage with the Prophet of Allah ﷺ was divinely ordained and the hypocrites words were meaningless.

*Madarij al-Nabuwwa*

---

The blessed wives of the Prophet ﷺ are mentioned in the Qur'an. They lived pious lives, always being satisfied with whatever Allah gave them.

• 274 •

# Long hands

Sayyida Aisha ؓ says that the wives of the Prophet ﷺ once asked him, "Who amongst us will be the first to follow you (in death)?" He replied, "Whoever has the longest hand among you."

The wives took a stick and began to measure each other's hand spans. The result being that Sayyida Sawdah's hand was physically the longest and biggest.

Sayyida Zaynab passed away first (amongst them) and they then came to realise that the meaning of the Prophet's statement was not the one with the longest palm and fingers, but the one who was most charitable in the way of Allah.

*Madarij al-Nabuwwa*

---

Being charitable and generous in the way of Allah leads to proximity to Allah and His Messenger ﷺ in this world and in the hereafter. Being charitable is the way of the Prophet, his family and his Companions (may Allah be pleased with them all).

• 275 •

# *Mother of the believers*
# Sayyida Safiyyah ﷺ

Sayyida Safiyyah ﷺ was the direct descendent of Sayyiduna Harun, the brother of Sayyiduna Musa ﷺ. She was the daughter of a chieftain. One night she had a dream in which she saw a brilliant moon that came in to her lap. She told her husband Kinanah about it. He got angry and slapped her so hard that a mark was left on her eye. In the battle of Khaybar, Kinanah was killed and Safiyyah was taken as a prisoner. Wahya asked for a woman slave and was given Safiyyah by the Prophet ﷺ. There were a lot of people in al-Madina who knew and had an affiliation with Safiyya's family and found it discomforting that she had become a servant. It was suggested that the Prophet should take her hand in marriage, as this move would make a lot of disgruntled people happy. The Prophet ﷺ decided to take this course of action and married her after compensating Wahya. The following morning after the Nikah the Prophet ﷺ told his Companions to bring whatever food they had with them and to come to his house. The Companions did as they were told and a small feast had been assembled. All the people ate this Walima. The Prophet ﷺ gave Safiyyah the choice of whether she wanted to return to her tribe in Khaybar or whether she was content with him in al-Madina. She heard this and said, "O Messenger of Allah! When I was in Khaybar I had dreams of being with you. How can I possibly leave you now?"

*Al-Muwahib Laduniyya*

---

Sayyida Safiyya's dream came true as she married the king of not only al-Madina but of all the worlds. We learn from this story that simplicity is the best policy. The walima of the Prophet ﷺ was a simple affair not the great extravagance that unfortunately most Muslims get involved in today. Fulfil the Sunnah, but in a simple manner.

• 276 •

# Daughter, niece and wife

One day Sayyida Hafsa said to Sayyida Safiyyah that you are the daughter of a Jew! Safiyyah started crying. The Prophet ﷺ heard about this and comforted his wife by telling her that she was the daughter, niece and wife of Prophets. You are the daughter of Harun ﷺ. The niece of Sayyiduna Musa ﷺ and above all you are my wife! You should be proud of this fact. The Prophet ﷺ then turned to his other wife Hafsa and said: 'Hafsa! Fear Allah and watch your tongue.'

*Mishkat Sharif*

---

We should never harm anyone by taunting them. The Prophet ﷺ rebuked Hafsa for doing so. This should be ample evidence for us not to do it to anybody.

The scholars of Hadith differ in regards to the total number of wives the Prophet ﷺ had. There is consensus on eleven wives, though some believe that there were more.

The eleven Mothers of the Faithful are:

**Sayyida Khadija**ﷺ

**Sayyida Aisha**ﷺ

**Sayyida Hafsa**ﷺ

**Sayyida Umm Habiba**ﷺ

**Sayyida Umm Salama**ﷺ

**Sayyida Sawdah**ﷺ

**Sayyida Zaynab bint Jahsh**ﷺ

**Sayyida Maymunah**ﷺ

**Sayyida Zaynab bint Khuzaymah**ﷺ

**Sayyida Juwayriyah bint al-Harith**ﷺ and

**Sayyida Safiyyah**ﷺ.

• 277 •

# Sayyida Fatima ﷺ

The Prophet ﷺ had four blessed daughters and of them the youngest and most beloved was Fatima ﷺ. One day Abdur-Rahman ibn Awf ﷺ saw the Holy Prophet ﷺ smile. He respectfully asked his master the reason why he was smiling. The Prophet replied that he had heard from the heavens that Allah has wished for the marriage of Ali to my daughter Fatima.

*Nuzahatul Majaalis*

Sayyida Fatima ﷺ holds a great honour and status and Islam. Her marriage with Ali was according to Allah's wishes.

# Marriage ceremony

When Sayyida Fatima had reached maturity, several offers for her hand in marriage came to the beloved Prophet. A Companion helped Ali to approach the Prophet for Fatima's hand in marriage. Abu Bakr Siddiq also helped Ali's cause. Ali having got the support of his friends went to the Prophet for Fatima's hand in marriage. But once he arrived there, he felt embarrassed and found it difficult to ask the Prophet. The Prophet noticed Ali's rather unusual appearance in his company and said, "Whatever you wish to say will be heard." Ali told the Prophet the reason for his visit. The Prophet heard this, smiled and said that his wish will be fulfilled. So on a pre-arranged date, Ali married Fatima in the Prophet's Mosque in al-Madina in front of the blessed Companions.

*Tarikh Islam*

The Companions of the Prophet lived such lives that they helped each other out whenever they needed help. The Companions all wished the marriage of Ali to Fatima with some, like Abu Bakr Siddiq, offering financial assistance. Allah, His Messenger and his Companions all wished this blessed marriage to go ahead.

# Fatima the bride

O believers! Listen carefully for this is the story of Fatima's marriage. She was a bride of fifteen years and Ali was twenty years old. Mawla Ali made an approach of marriage that the Prophet accepted. It was on Monday seventeenth Rajab in the second year of Hijra in al-Madina that a public announcement was made that after Zuhr everyone was invited to the ceremony. A great buzz received this news in every house, street and market. This was no ordinary day for it was the marriage of Mawla Ali and Fatima Zahra. The time of Zuhr arrived and all the Companions gathered at the Prophet's mosque. Abu Bakr, Umar were sitting on one side, Uthman and others were also present. Wherever one looked Ansars and Muhajirs were present, and amongst them was Ahmad-e- Mukhtar. The assembled waited in anticipation. When Prophet Muhammad completed the sermon the knot between Ali and Zahra was tied. Four hundred dinars silver was the Mahr, the weight of which was 150 tola. Mouth-watering dates were brought forth. Except for this there was nothing else to eat. A supplication (dua) was made after that. Congratulations were given to one and all. When the time for departure came for the bride in memory of her mother she began to cry. Ahmad-e-Mukhtar comforted her and then said to her, "You are good and fortunate in every respect, of all relatives you are best. Your father is Imam of the prophets! And Ali is the chief of the saints." In the month of Dhu'l Hajj a dinner took place in which there was dry bread and dates to eat. This is what they call a Walima. This invitation is the Sunnah of the Prophet.

*Islami Zindagi*

---

This story narrated by Maulana Mufti Ahmad Yaar Khan was originally in the form of a poem. At the end he concludes:

**Everyone should follow this path**
**And avoid bad habits and customs.**

# Bride's dowry

The day Sayyida Fatimaﷺ got married she received the following things in her dowry:

A shawl with seventeen patches on it given by the Messenger of Allahﷺ

A leather skin mattress to sleep on

A pillow and quilt in which there was neither silk or cotton. But was instead full of bits of bark and skin.

A millstone (to grind flour)

A leather water bag

A wooden bowl

A silver bracelet

A necklace made of elephant's teeth

A suit

*Islami Zindagi*

The Beloved of Allahﷺ is the master of both worlds. He could have wished whatever he wanted. But for himself and his family he chose simplicity and this is reflected in the dowry of Fatimaﷺ.

# Tasbih of Fatima

Sayyida Fatima᷊ took on all the domestic duties when she moved in to the home of Mawla Ali after their wedding. Her clothes would get dirty and blisters would appear on her hands as she did the millstone. One day she informed her husband Ali that the Prophet᷊ was allocating house servants and that he should go and try get one for their house. Fatima went and pleaded with him to offer her assistance and relief in her new home. She began showing the blisters on her hands to him. The Prophet kept quiet. That evening the Prophet᷊ went to Fatima's house. He told her that the house servants were for those people who lost male members of the house in battle. But he gave her a daughter a valuable invocation. Recite Alhamdulillah 33 times, Subhanallah 33 times and Allahu-Akbar 34 times every night before going to bed. Such a *tasbih* removes any physical tiredness from the body. Sayyida Fatima᷊ learnt it and became happy.

*Islami Zindagi*

---

The Prophet᷊ offered his daughter the best of help to relieve her from her problems. From that day on Fatima did not complain to anyone as she had now found a solution by invoking and glorifying Allah the Almighty. Allah says in the Qur'an "They are those who have believed and their hearts find satisfaction with the remembrance of Allah. Behold! In the remembrance of Allah alone is their satisfaction of hearts." (Raad 28).

# Suit from heaven

A daughter of a rich Jewish man in al-Madina was getting married. Many of the women of the city were invited to this prestigious event. The women who were very rich suggested that they invite Fatima ﷺ to the wedding. They wished to show how beautiful their clothes were compared to Fatima. The girls sent out an invitation to Fatima to which she sought the permission of her beloved Prophet ﷺ before giving an answer. Sayyiduna Jibreel ﷺ appeared in front of the Prophet ﷺ with a beautiful suit for Fatima that was from Paradise. The Prophet ﷺ called his beloved daughter and told her that she could attend the wedding and that she should wear this suit. She wore the suit and went to the wedding. She arrived and sat quietly not disturbing anyone. But the suit she wore was so beautiful and so shining that everyone's attention was towards Fatima and not the bride. They asked Fatima, "Where did you get such a beautiful suit?" (They never anticipated her having such fine clothes) Fatima said, "This has come from my father's house." "And which house is that?" the women asked. "Paradise" replied Fatima. "And who gave this suit to your father?" Sayyida Fatima ﷺ said, "Jibreel." The women were so astonished that they accepted Islam and became good friends of Fatima, the first lady of Paradise.

*Nuzahatul Majaalis*

---

The Prophet ﷺ and his family have chosen the state of poverty out of choice. They preferred simplicity to everything else. If they wished as this story amply illustrates they could have whatever they wish directly from Paradise.

# A great invitation

One day Sayyiduna Uthman invited the Prophet to his home. He accepted and went with his Companions to Uthman's house. Sayyiduna Uthman began to count every footstep of the Prophet. The Prophet noticed this asked him what he was doing. Uthman proudly replied that he wished to free a slave for every blessed step he took from the Mosque to his house in happiness of the fact that the Prophet was coming to his house for dinner. After the dinner, Sayyiduna Ali returned home in a baffled state. Fatima noticed Ali's strange mood and asked him what the matter was? Ali told his wife that Uthman held an invitation for the Prophet in which he promised to free a slave for every step the Prophet took from the Mosque to his house. The dinner he served was excellent in which there was every dish. "It is at times like these that I wish we were richer so that we could serve the Prophet like how Uthman and many other Companions do." Fatima could not bear to see him in this state anymore and told him to go and invite the Prophet of Allah for dinner tomorrow. Ali went and invited the Prophet. Sayyida Fatima fell into prostration to Allah and asked Him to hear her plea. She asked Allah to save her and her father's honour by helping her provide for an excellent dinner. She finished her plea when she went into the kitchen to start cooking. She again started pleading with Allah to save her grace. Allah heard her heartfelt plea and sent food from Paradise. She thanked Allah as she then began giving the food out. The Prophet was eating the delicious food when he asked his noble Companions whether they knew where the food they were eating came from. The Companions out of respect asked the Prophet to answer his own question. "This food is from Paradise! Allah has sent it for you today." The Companions were ecstatic to hear this. Fatima was still not satisfied. She went in prayer and said, "O

Allah! Uthman decided to free a slave for every footstep of the Messenger ﷺ to his house. Your slave Fatima does not have that much wealth. O Allah just as you sent food from Paradise when I had no food, then please set free a Muslim destined for Hell fire and place him in Paradise for every footstep the Master of both worlds took from the Mosque to my house." Fatima had barely finished the prayer when Jibreel عليه السلام appeared in the holy presence of the Messenger of Allah with the good news that Allah has decided that your daughter's prayer has been accepted by her Lord and that for every step you took in reaching this house Allah has ordered the freeing of one thousand sinners from Hell and be placed in Paradise. The Prophet ﷺ conveyed this message to Fatima and the Companions who became even more ecstatic.

*Jami al-Mujizaat*

---

For the sake of Sayyida Fatima ﷺ Allah sent food from Paradise to her house so that the Prophet of Allah and his Companions could enjoy a wonderful feast. Furthermore thousands of sinful Muslims have been pardoned on account of every footstep of the Beloved of Allah to his beloved dauughter's house. The Companions of the Prophet of Allah were not jealous of each other but competed with one another in good deeds. The Noble Companions loved the family of the Prophet and gave them their due respect. Allah is pleased with them all.

• 284 •

# Secret conversation

The *Mother of the Believers* Sayyida Aisha ﷺ says that when the Holy Prophet ﷺ was in his final illness, he said something to his beloved daughter Sayyida Fatima Zahra ﷺ which made her cry but a few seconds later the Prophet ﷺ said something in her ear that made her smile and giggle. Sayyida Aisha noticed this and asked Fatima what was said but Fatima would not tell her.

After the Prophet ﷺ left this mortal world, Aisha again asked Fatima about the secret conversation that day. "Why did you cry when the Prophet said something and why did you then smile at the second comment?" Fatima said, "O Mother! The Prophet ﷺ told me that Sayyiduna Jibreel عليه السلام came this Ramadan and recited the entire Qur'an to me twice rather than the customary once. He knew that his death was near. This is what made me cry. Then the Prophet ﷺ said to me that the first person to greet me from my family would be me. So I smiled and felt relieved at the news that the pain of separation would be a short one. That is why I smiled."

*Sahih al-Bukhari*

---

Sayyida Fatima ﷺ holds a unique and unparalleled place of love and affection in the heart of our Prophet ﷺ. He knew that his death was near and he also knew that his beloved daughter would follow him.

• 285 •

# Sayyida Fatima's worldy departure

The Prophet of Allah left this mortal word in Rabi al-Awwal 11 Hijri. From that moment on, Fatima wept and remained in a sad state and always yearned to be with her father again. In Ramadan 11 AH, she sensed her time was near and she called her husband Mawla Ali and requested him to be ever caring over her two stars – Hasan and Husayn. As the time approached, she said 'Ali! Behold the Prophet of Allah is coming, my time of union with my Lord is near! After my soul departs, I have left a letter in a certain place, please place it in my grave." Ali asked, "What is written on this piece of paper? For the sake of the Prophet ﷺ please tell me." "When my marriage to you was taking place the Prophet ﷺ told me that he was arranging my marriage to you in exchange for four hundred dinars of silver. I told the Prophet ﷺ that I accept Ali but not the dowry. In that time Jibreel عليه السلام came with the message that Allah says that Paradise and all its blessings have been established as Fatima's dowry. The Prophet ﷺ told me this and made me became happy. The Prophet ﷺ then asked me what the dowry should be? (i.e. Jannat is at your disposal, how will you use it?) I replied O Messenger of Allah! At every moment you are thinking about your Ummah. I wish that the forgiveness of your sinful believers is made as my dowry." A piece of paper was brought forward on which it was written

**"The intercession of the Ummah of Muhammad ﷺ is Fatima's dowry"**

*Jami' al-Mujizaat*

The intercession of the Prophet's Ummah is guaranteed otherwise the Nikah of Ali and Fatima will remain incomplete. Fatima ﷺ was always attentive to the Prophet's wishes. We also learn that we should not cry excessively or scream at the time of death or despair, but should remain steadfast and patient.

• 286 •

# Ali and the Kufi troops

Mawla Ali ﷺ as Caliph of the Muslims called upon the people of Kufa to send troops. Before the army from Kufa had arrived Ali told his men that the army would contain 12,000 men. A companion of Ali heard this and decided to count the Kufi troops when they arrived. He was amazed to discover that there were exactly 12,000 troops present.

*Shawahid al-Nabuwwa*

The knowledge and wisdom Ali possesed was due to the honour and blessings of the Prophet ﷺ. Who then can place a limit to the knowledge the Prophet ﷺ? Yet people today have the audacity to say that the Prophet has no knowledge. Such people are in fact themselves ignorant.

• 287 •

# House purchase contract

A man seeking to buy a house came to Sayyiduna Ali ؓ asking him to write up a suitable contract for the property. Ali requested to the man to listen to what he had to say before he agreed to the terms of the contract. This is what he said:

"This is a house where a man suffers and makes others suffer. The house will not survive and neither will the occupant. The house is on a street where forgetful people (of the hereafter) live. There are four limits to it. The first limit is death, the second is the grave, the third is the Day of Judgement and the fourth- heaven or Hell -is still unknown." The man listened attentively and began to cry as he left in a state of shock. The man refused to buy the house.

*Seerat al-Salihin*

The world and its inhabitants will one day perish. It is therefore imperative that we make preparations for the infinitely lasting hereafter. One should continually remember the grave, the day of rising and the hereafter by knowing the bliss of Paradise and the punishment and fire of Hell.

# Box of deeds

A man named Kameel was once accompanying Ali when they passed a graveyard. Ali stopped and began to address the people of the grave and said, "O people of the grave! O lonely people! What news do you have? What is the state in your graves? The news is this. Your wealth has been distributed amongst the living, your children are orphaned and your wives have married other men. This is our state tell us about yours?" Mawla Ali looked at me and said, "Kameel! If these people were allowed to speak (by Allah) then the response to my questions would be that the best provision for the journey of life is Taqwa (God-fear)." Ali started to weep a lot and said, "O Kameel! The grave is a box that possesses your deeds. It's only when you get there do you realise what you have done."

*Hujjatullah ala'l Alamin*

After we die everything remains in the world. Others then gain hold of the wealth we used to own. The only exception is our good actions, which we need to increase if we are to have a successful and peaceful journey in the hereafter.

# Ali's physique

One day Mawla Aliﷺ was walking along when two tall Companions joined him. Mawla Ali was of medium short build, and looked smaller compared to the two tall men. One of the Companions said to Ali in a light-hearted manner, "O Ali! You are like the 'noon' in 'Lana' as my friend and I am tall like 'Laam' and 'Alif'. Ali responded by saying, "If I was not here then you would become 'La' i.e. 'no' because removing the 'noon' from 'lana' makes 'La' which is to be non-existent, to be extinct and annihilated."

*Mughni al-Wa'izin*

---

The Companions loved each other very much and would joke with each other in a lighthearted and sensible manner. The Prophet ﷺ united the hearts and minds of the People of Arabia and this is typified with light humour. This story amply illustrates Mawla Ali's quick thinking and wisdom. There is no doubt that without Ali we would become 'La' i.e. non-existent and annihilated.

• 290 •

# Examination

A polytheist appeared before Mawla Ali ؑ with a bizarre challenge. He challenged Ali that if your Lord is who he says He is then, he should climb up onto the roof and call out His name and then jump and see if he remains alive. The man wanted to see whether his Lord would save him from certain death. Ali heard this and told the hopeless man that his comment proved his stupidity. "Do you want me to test Allah who is the Almighty and all powerful?"

*Mathnawi Sharif*

---

It is a sign of stupidity and idiocy that a person would wish to challenge Allah who is free from all wants and needs.

# Answer to problem

One day a person came to him and stated that a human is all-powerful and can do as he pleases (which was the belief of an early sect called the Qadariyya). Ali ordered, "Lift one of your legs up and stand on the other." The person did as instructed. Then Ali said, "Leave this leg raised and lift the second leg up." The person replied, "If I try that I will fall to the ground." In response, Ali said, "It is just this much free-will which humans possess. If man was all-powerful, he would be able to raise both feet in the standing position."

*Manzoom*

---

Though he says that he does everything on his own account, the reality is that it is Allah who is the real operator of everything. Man has many qualities but he is also defective and extremely unstable.

• 292 •

# Sayyiduna Imam Hasan

The Prophet of Allah was climbing up the pulpit to deliver the Khutba when his beloved grandchild Imam Hasan entered the Mosque. The Prophet during the Khutba would look at the Noble Companions and then look just at Imam Hasan. The Messenger of Allah addressing the Companions said of

Imam Hasan that, "O Companions! This (grand) son of mine is a leader and will reunite the Muslims into one group."

*Mishkat Sharif*

---

The Prophet❀ demonstrates his knowledge of the unseen – ilm al-ghayb – in this account. The story in question refers to events after the death of Mawla Ali❀. After the martyrdom of Ali in Kufa, Imam Hasan assumed the title and role of 'Amir al-Muminin'. A group however supported Amir Muawiya❀ and demanded his position as the Leader of the Muslims. After six months, Imam Hasan after securing an agreement with Amir Muawiya gave up the Caliphate in favour of the Governor of Damascus. This move resulted in the re-reunion of the Muslims under one banner. Imam Hasan thus averted a serious civil war amongst the Muslims at that particular time. We learn from the account narrated in *Mishkat* above that the Prophet❀ knew who would take charge of the Muslims after he left this world. The Prophet's words indicate quite clearly that Amir Muawiya was leader of the Muslims as Imam Hasan united two large Muslim groups. Amir Muawiya is amongst the most prominent of Companions. It is therefore not permissible to say anything bad against him or to criticise him. If he were on the 'wrong path' then Imam Hasan would have definitely opposed him just as his younger brother Imam al-Husayn opposed Amir Muawiya's son Yazid.

• 293 •

# One hundred and fifty thousand dinars

Amir Muawiya gave Sayyiduna Imam Hasan a sum of one hundred thousand dinars per annum. One year a delay took place in the payment, which caused Imam Hasan some difficulties. Imam Hasan wanted to complain to Amir Muawiya and ordered a pen and paper but after thinking about it carefully, he did not write the letter of complaint. One night, Imam Hasan saw the Holy Prophet❀ in his dream. The Prophet❀ spoke to him asking how he was? He informed his grandfather about the delay in payment. The Prophet❀ said, "You ordered the ink and paper so you could write the complaint." "O Messenger of Allah! I was forced to. What else could I do?" The Prophetﷺ then told Imam Hasan to read a dua. Imam Hasan says that after that particular meeting with the Prophetﷺ a week later a payment of one hundred and fifty thousand was made to him. Imam Hasan thanked Allah immensely for the payment. Imam Hasan again met the Prophetﷺ in his dream and said, "O Hasan! How are you?" Hasan replied by praising Allah and then told the Prophet about the increased payment. The Prophetﷺ replied, "What you ask from your Lord, the reward is only valued in the next world."

*Tarikh al-Khulafa*

---

It was respect and honour for Imam Hasan that compelled Amir Muawiya to give him an annual amount, especially a large sum like this. A delay in payment compelled him to pay extra by fifty thousand, showing the open generosity and sincerity of Amir Muawiya. By accepting the payment, we learn that Imam Hasan recognised the rule of Amir Muawiya otherwise he would have never accepted the payment from him.

• 294 •

# Excellent passenger

One day the Prophetﷺ took his darling and beloved grandson Imam Hasan and placed him on top of his shoulders in such a way that the tiny legs of Imam Hasan rested on each of the Prophet's blessed shoulders. He was walking along when a companion saw this beautiful sight and said, "O Hasan! What an excellent conveyance you have taking you." The Prophetﷺ responded, "But look at how excellent the passenger is."

*Tarikh al-Khulafa*

The Prophet ﷺ absolutely adored children and played with them a lot. His love for his two grandsons' exemplifies and illustrates this point. The Prophet ﷺ took every opportunity to tell his followers that his family was the best and that they should be loved and respected accordingly.

• 295 •

# Servant's slip

One day Sayyiduna Imam Hasan ﷺ had invited a few guests for dinner. His servant was bringing some curry for them when it slipped out of his hands and fell on the floor. Some of the curry went on the clothes of Imam Hasan. The servant saw what had happened and became scared at what might happen to him. Imam Hasan looked towards him when the servant read the verse, "And those who drink anger." Imam Hasan replied, "I have drunk my anger." The servant then said, "And those people who pardon mistakes" from the Qur'an. Imam Hasan told his servant, "Go! I have forgiven you." He then said, "Indeed Allah loves those who do (Good) Ihsan."

*Ruh al-Bayan*

We should try and avoid being angry and be as forgiving as possible to everyone. Anger is a vice that does immense damage.

# Generous household

Sayyiduna Imam Hasan﷿, Imam al-Husayn﷿ and Abdullah ibn Ja'far﷿ once went for Hajj. A camel they had for their provisions got tired and was left behind during the journey. The brothers became thirsty and hungry and stopped at a house where an old woman lived. They entered the house and asked the lady whether they could have something to drink. The lady responded by milking her goat and offered the fresh milk to the young men. After drinking the milk to quench their thirst, they asked the lady whether she had anything to eat. The lady keen to serve her guests slaughtered her goat and cooked the meat and fed it to them. After eating the meal, the three men told the old lady that they were from Quraysh and they would – Allah willing – reward her fully for the hospitality she showed. The men left for Makkah with the lady not fully aware who these young men were. Her husband arrived from work to find their only goat slaughtered. He rebuked his wife for giving their only goat to some strangers who they were unlikely to meet ever again.

The brothers successfully completed their Hajj and returned to al-Madina. It was a few months after the incident, when the couple went to al-Madina in search for some camels and provisions. Imam Hasan﷿ saw the lady and recognised her. He went up to her and asked her if she recognised and remembered him. The old lady apologised for not knowing who he was. Imam Hasan﷿ reminded the lady about her hospitality. She heard all this and remembered. As promised, Imam Hasan﷿ told the lady that she would be rewarded for the service she did for them that day. Imam Hasan﷿ ordered that one thousand goats and one thousand dinars be given to the lady. Imam Hasan﷿ after giving the provisions to the lady took her with his servant to the house of Imam al-Husayn﷿ where Imam Hasan﷿ prompted his younger brother about her. Imam al-Husaynﷺ asked the lady what his elder brother had given her? She replied that she was given one thousand goats and one thousand dinars. Imam al-Husaynﷺ ordered that the same number of goats and dinars be given to the guest. Imam al-Husaynﷺ with his servant then took the lady to the house of Abdullah ibn Ja'farﷺ. Sayyiduna Ja'farﷺ asked the lady what the two brothers had given her? She replied that the two brothers had given her two thousand goats and two thousand dinars. He heard this and ordered that the lady be given another two thousand goats and two thousand dinars. The lady left al-Madina that day with four thousand goats and four thousand dinars, all this reward for serving one goat to the Ahl al-Bayt.

*Kimiy al-Sa'adat*

---

The Ahl al-Bayt is the household of generosity. The lady without knowing who they were served them and offered hospitality towards them. She was rewarded immensely as a result. So what would be the reward for those Muslims who know the status and honour of the Ahl al-Bayt and do *Esale-e-Sawab* upon their souls? Would they not get immense benefits in this world and in the hereafter?

• 297 •

## Priceless drink

Sayyiduna Imam Hasanﷺ once had a guest at his house. The guest after eating asked his host for a drink. Imam Hasanﷺ asked his guest what type of drink he was looking for? The guest replied that he wanted such a drink that was worth more than life when not receiving it, and at the point of receiving is worth a lot less. Imam Hasanﷺ heard this and told his servant to bring a glass of water. The guest was amazed at the wisdom and swiftness of his host's response.

Water is one of Allah's greatest favours and without which our living would be unbearable. Shaykh Saadi notes that when a chicken drinks a sip of water, it immediately then lifts its head towards the sky in thanks to its creator for giving it a drink. Man, on the other hand, who has been endowed with intelligence above and beyond all animals, drinks water till he is full and does not thank Allah at all. Is the ungrateful man any better than an animal?

• 298 •

# Bloody face

A man was arrested and brought in front of Mawla Ali. He was found in some wastelands on the outskirts of the city possessing a blood stained knife standing over a corpse. He admitted guilt and awaited the verdict from Mawla Ali.

In that time another man came running in the court of Ali claiming he was the murderer. Perplexed by the unfolding events, Mawla Ali asked the first man to explain his case. He said, "It is pointless for me to claim my innocence. No one will believe me. I had a blood stained knife in my possession standing over him." Mawla Ali was unsatisfied and wanted elaboration. The accused continued, "I am a butcher. I was out there slaughtering some goats and sheep. I desperately needed to go and relieve myself so I went and did so. On my return, I spotted the corpse and went over to investigate. In that time people saw me and from then I knew I was in trouble."

Mawla Ali then asked the second man to explain his story. He said, "I am a poor man and out of desperation and need for money I killed the man. I heard some footsteps and hid behind a bush. This man stood before us was there and in no time at all he was being arrested for a crime he did not commit. This is what brings me here. He is innocent and not guilty."

Mawla Ali paused and then turned to his son Imam Hasan and asked for his opinion on what should be done. Imam Hasan replied, "O leader of the faithful! If this person has committed a heinous crime by killing someone he has also however saved a life by sparing an innocent man from certain death. Allah states that whoever saves one life is as if they have saved the entire mankind." Mawla Ali liked this view and decided to forgive the murderer. Blood money was then given to the murdered family from the Bayt al Maal (Public Treasury).

*Al Tarq al Hakmiya*

---

A Qazi or judge has to pay full and undivided attention during a case. He must deliver the case with rationality and sincerity. We learn from this story that Imam Hasan possessed great wisdom and foresight. We learn that decisions are not diminished in any way if people make them younger in age. Sayyiduna Umar the Caliph would often approach Ali, who was younger than him, for help on decisions he could not resolve by himself. We also find precedence with the previous prophets (peace be upon them) as Sayyiduna Dawud asked his son Sulaiman to decide cases.

• 299 •

# Heavenly apple

Imam Hasan and Imam al-Husayn were drawing some pictures and began to ask each other whose picture was better? They decided to go and ask their father Mawla Ali. Ali saw their pictures and told them to go and asked their beloved mother Sayyida Fatima Zahra. She saw the drawings and said that Sayyiduna Muhammad should make the decision. Both boys approached the Messenger of Allah and sought his opinion. Sayyiduna Muhammad ﷺ smiled and told his two darling grandsons that Sayyiduna Jibreel ؏ will come from the heavens and decide. Jibreel ؏ appeared in front of the Prophet ﷺ and told him that he could not make the decision, but that Allah will make the decision himself. Jibreel ؏ returned from Paradise with an apple. He was ordered to place the apple on their slates. On whichever slate the apple remains, that slate would be deemed the better drawing. By Allah's will and command the single apple split into two and stayed on both slates. Allah had decided that both drawings were equally good and that they were both winners.

Nuzahatul Majaalis

---

Imam Hasan and al-Husayn hold a special and unique place in the hearts and minds of the Ahl al-Bayt and its followers. Allah and his angels wish for their happiness. It is only right that we should do the same and love and respect the two Imams as Allah, His Prophet and angels do.

• 300 •

# Angel's duty

Imam Hasan and al-Husayn ؏ went to play outside. It had been a while since they had gone out playing when Sayyida Fatima ؏ became anxious about them. The Prophet of Allah ﷺ in this time appeared at the house of his beloved daughter. Fatima told the Messenger of Allah ﷺ that they had gone out to play and had not returned and that she did not know where they were. Sayyiduna Jibreel ؏ appeared in the holy presence of the Prophet and informed him that his beloved grandsons were still playing at a certain place and that angels were guarding them. The Prophet of Allah then went to fetch the boys. He arrived there to see the two boys sleeping. He saw an angel guarding them as they slept. The Prophet of Allah픿 picked the two boys up kissed them and took them back home to their worried mother.

*Nuzahatul Majaalis*

---

We learn from this that it is the duty of the angels to protect the Ahl al-Bayt at all times. No sooner had Sayyida Fatima informed the Prophet픿 about the boys, Allah sent Jibreel픿 the most senior of angels to go and inform them about their whereabouts. If angels respect and guard the Ahl al-Bayt then it is imperative on us, the Ummati of the Prophet, to uphold their honour and sanctity for the best family.

• 301 •

# Cure for thirst

One day the Prophet픿 heard screaming and crying come from the house of Fatima and Ali. He ran towards the house to enquire as to why his beloved grandsons were crying? Fatima픿 informed the Messenger픿 that her sons were thirsty and that she had ran out of water. He픿 told his daughter to bring his beloved grandsons towards him. The Prophet픿 picked up Imam Hasan and told him to suck his blessed tongue. Hasan did so and sucked on it until he was no longer thirsty, and stopped crying. The Prophet픿 then picked up his darling al-Husayn and did the same with him. al-Husayn sucked on the truthful tongue of the Prophet until he was satisfied.

*Hujjatullah Ala'l Alamin*

---

The Prophet of Allah픿 could not bear to see his darling grandsons in anguish and the same applied after the Prophet픿 left this world. Whoever hurts or harms the Ahl al-Bayt has hurt the Prophet픿. And whoever hurts or harms the Prophet픿 then they will have to answer to Allah. And against Allah there is no help.

• 302 •

# Awe and bravery

One day Sayyida Fatima went with Imam Hasan and al-Husayn to Sayyiduna Muhammad to ask for something for her two sons. "O Messenger of Allah! Please give them something." The Prophet accepted his daughter's plea and gave Hasan his knowledge and awe and al-Husayn was given bravery and graciousness.

*Ibn Asakir, Al amn wal Ulaa*

---

Imam Hasan and Imam al-Husayn have been bestowed with awe and bravery, knowledge and generosity. These things were granted directly, by Allah's will, by the Prophet of Allah. We learn from this that the treasures of everything Allah has created are in the possession of the Messenger who is Qasim- the distributor- and it is he who distributes to whoever he wills.

• 303 •

# A strange dream

One night Imam Hasan in his dream saw the verse of the Qur'an "Say (O Prophet!) Allah is one," written between his two eyes. The next morning he asked his family whether they could explain to him the meaning of this strange dream. Sa'id ibn al-Musayyib told Imam Hasan that the meaning of his dream was that he would leave this mortal world. A few days after the dream, Imam Hasan died after being poisoned.

*Tarikh al-Khulafa*

38

Imam Hasan was informed in his dream of his impending death. The people of knowledge should be asked about the meaning of dreams.

• 304 •

# Martydom

The enemies of Ahl al-Bayt plotted against the innocent Imam Hasan even after he gave up power in favour of Amir Muawiya. They tried to kill him by poisoning him. The poisoned food caused him severe diarrhoea. This purging of the bowels caused him severe pain for forty days. Close to his last breath, his younger brother Imam al-Husayn appeared to hear his last words. Imam al-Husayn asked Imam Hasan who poisoned him? Imam Hasan asked his brother whether he would go and kill the person who did it? Imam al-Husayn told his brother that he would. Imam Hasan told his younger brother that if he was poisoned, then Allah the Almighty who is the greatest and real avenger (*Muntaqim Haqeeqi*) would be sufficient to gain justice, and that if he was not poisoned he did not wish to spill innocent blood spilt in his name and cause further tensions in the Ummah.

*Tarikh al-Khulafa*

Imam Hasan on his deathbed displayed a true sense of justice and God fear in that he did not reveal to his younger brother his murderer lest that innocent blood was spilt for his sake. Imam Hasan displayed true faith in Allah knowing that Allah would destroy his murderer in this world and in the hereafter.

• 305 •

# Sayyiduna Imam al-Husayn ﷺ

Umme Fadl, wife of Abbas ﷺ says that one night she had a dream in which a piece of the Prophet of Allah ﷺ fell into her lap. She was surprised by this dream and went and told the Prophet about it. She said, "O Messenger of Allah! I saw a strange dream in which a piece of you came into my lap." Sayyiduna Muhammad ﷺ said, "Your dream is a very good one, because Fatima ﷺ will have a child who will play in your lap." Hence Sayyida Fatima gave birth to Imam al-Husayn ﷺ who played in the lap of Umme Fadl ﷺ.

*Mishkat Sharif*

Imam al-Husayn ﷺ was the darling of our Prophet. To love Imam al-Husayn is to love the Prophet, and hatred for him, is to have hatred for the Prophet.

• 306 •

# Sayyiduna Imam al-Husayn ﷺ and a Bedouin

A Bedouin appeared before Imam al-Husayn ﷺ and said to him, "I have heard from your noble grandfather, the Prophet of Prophets, Sayyiduna Muhammad ﷺ that when a person has a request or a desire, he should go to one of four persons. Either he should go to a noble Arab man, a noble leader, a Hafiz of the Qur'an or a graceful and beautiful person. "O al-Husayn! This is because the Arabs have attained nobility and respect because of your family and generosity is your philosophy. As for the Qur'an, this manifest book was revealed in your house and in regards to your charm and beauty, I have heard from the Holy Prophet ﷺ himself that if you wish to see and remember me than look at Imam Hasan or Imam al-Husayn."

Imam al-Husayn ؑ asked the Bedouin what he wanted? The Bedouin wrote on the ground what he desired. Imam al-Husayn ؑ said to the Bedouin, "I have heard from my noble grandfather that good deeds are gained in lieu of recognition. So I will ask you three questions. If you get one question right I will give you one third of what you desire. And if you give two right answers then two-thirds is yours, and if all three are right then all you desire will be given in full." The Bedouin agreed and awaited the first of three questions. The first question was that of all acts, which is the most excellent? The Bedouin replied, "To believe in Allah." Imam then asked what thing saves one from destruction and annihilation. The Bedouin replied to have *tawakkul* (complete trust) in Allah. Imam al-Husayn ؑ asked him that from what thing does one gain beauty? The Bedouin replied that it is from knowledge that one gets beauty as one gets patience and tolerance from it. Imam asked, "And what if someone does not have that virtue? The Bedouin replied that the person should have wealth, which is used charitably. Imam said, "And what if someone does not have wealth?" The petitioner replied that the person needs a bolt of lightning! Imam al-Husayn laughed at this last response and happily gave the Bedouin what he asked for.

*Nuzahatul Majaalis*

---

To seek help from the friends of Allah is to act according to the words of the Holy Prophet ﷺ. Furthermore the friends of Allah fulfil the requests of their petitioners. Nobody leaves empty handed. We learn that Imam al-Husayn was a very generous person and that the Bedouins of the earlier times had knowledge and recognition (*Marifat*) of the truth.

# The scent of Karbala

One day, Imam al-Husayn was in the lap of the Messenger. Umme Fazl was sitting next to them. She saw the Prophet with tears in his eyes. She asked, "O Messenger of Allah! Why the tears?" The Prophet said, "Sayyiduna Jibreel has just come to me and told me that this son of mine will be killed by my Ummah. Jibreel has presented to me the soil of the place where he will be martyred." The Prophet of Allah smelt the soil and handed it over to Umm Salama and said, "O Umm Salama! Keep this soil with you. One day this soil will turn into blood. When that happens, my son will have been martyred." Umm Salama kept this soil in a glass jar. When Imam al-Husayn was martyred on the tenth of Muharram that jar of soil turned into blood.

*Mishkat Sharif, Hujjatullah ala'l Alamin*

The Holy Prophet had knowledge that his beloved son Imam al-Husayn would be martyred and also the place where it would happen. The Prophet of Allah also knew that Umm Salama would still be alive when Karbala would take place and gave the soil to her. If somebody then says that He did not have knowledge of the unseen, then how ignorant are these people?

# A bold response

In Rajab 60AH, Amir Muawiyya ﷺ passed away. His son Yazid took over the Caliphate. To ensure the recognition of his office, he sent letters throughout the Islamic lands to gain approval and an oath of allegiance (*Bay'a*) from all the Muslims. A letter was sent to al-Madina to the Governor so that the people of al-Madina did the same. Yazid desperately wanted Imam al-Husayn to recognise and legitimise his leadership. The Governor of al-Madina went to Imam al-Husayn and told him what Yazid wanted. Imam al-Husayn ﷺ because of Yazid's record of adultery, wickedness and impiety refused to recognise him as the leader of the Muslims and with full conviction told the Governor that under no circumstances would he recognise his Caliphate. When Yazid was informed of Imam al-Husayn's bold response he became very angry.

*Sirrul Shahadatayn, Saniha e Karbala al-Sadrulal- Faazil*

---

Yazid was an adulterer and a wicked person who lacked piety. It was because of these vices that Imam al-Husayn ﷺ refused to swear an oath of allegiance. We learn from his bold response that he was the son of a brave man, Sayyiduna Mawla Ali (may Allah be pleased with him). Imam al-Husayn ﷺ knew that refusing to recognise Yazid would provoke and incite him and that he would be willing to spill blood to achieve his aims. Imam al-Husayn after speaking out the truth did not try to flee to protect himself. So how could it possibly be that his father the Lion of Allah (*Assadullah*) did not display bravery and courage when speaking out the truth?

# In the presence of the Prophet

When Yazid found out that Imam al-Husayn﷤ would not swear allegiance to him, he in a state of irritation and frustration sent a message to the Governor of al-Madina, that Imam al-Husayn﷤ would be forced to swear allegiance to him otherwise his head would be chopped off and presented to Yazid. When Imam al-Husayn﷤ found out that the sanctity of al-Madina was at risk, he decided to leave the City of the Prophet and migrate to Makkah.

On the eve of his forced migration, Imam al-Husayn﷤ presented himself to the Prophet of Mercyﷺ. He cried and wept as he told his Holy grandfather about his predicament. In the shadow of the Prophet's tomb (*Rawda*), Imam al-Husayn﷤ fell asleep. In his dream, the Prophet visited him and kissed and embraced him. He said, "O al-Husayn! Soon the oppressors will trouble you in Karbala and kill you. Your mother, father and elder brother are eagerly awaiting you in Paradise. There is a place for you here in Allah's presence, which cannot be attained without being martyred. O son! Accept martyrdom with patience and gratitude to Allah."

Imam al-Husayn﷤ woke up from his dream and went home and told his family about his dream. He made firm his commitment to leave al-Madina for Makkah. He with his family went to the *Rawda* and presented their salaams to the Prophet of Mercyﷺ. Imam al-Husayn﷤ then went to his mother's grave and said, "O mother! Your son is being made to separate from you today." A voice came from the grave, which said, "Salaams upon you O oppressed!" Imam al-Husayn﷤ heard this and wept at his mother's side. With tears in his eyes he bid farewell to his mother and set off for Makkah.

*Tazkirah al-Husayn*

Imam al-Husayn knew very well that he was to be martyred in Karbala. His exemplary upbringing made him prepared for the levels of patience and perseverance needed for this stern test. And despite knowing that, he displayed a great sense of perseverance and commitment to being martyred. The life of Imam al-Husayn tells us that seeking Allah's pleasure means being subservient to His will. By following Allah's will, Imam al-Husayn found peace and comfort. Imam al-Husayn was not scared with what was about to happen. Indeed he was waiting for the hour he would be sacrificed.

• 310 •

# The letters from Kufa

When the people of Iraq learnt that Imam al-Husayn had refused to swear an oath of allegiance to Yazid, they then began to send letters to Imam al-Husayn who had by now left al-Madina for Makkah. They invited him to come and stay in Iraq so that they could challenge Yazid who was in Damascus, Syria. They promised to swear an oath to Imam al-Husayn and fight with him against Yazid. Approximately one hundred and fifty letters of this nature came from Kufa, which pleaded with al-Husayn ibn Ali to come to Kufa. It was such an overwhelming appeal by the Kufan's that he could not afford to ignore. So Imam al-Husayn decided to send his cousin Muslim ibn Aqeel to assess the situation in Kufa. If he reported back to say that the people of Kufa were genuine and sincere then he would travel but if they were not, then he would remain in Makkah.

*Sirrul Shahadatayn, Saniha e Karbala Tazkirah, al-Husayn*

Despite the people of Kufa being infamously treacherous and faithless, Imam al-Husayn responded to their pleas. And there was good reason for him to do so. Because on the Day of Judgement Allah could have asked the people of Kufa why they did *Bay'a* of Yazid? They could have said that they called the grandson of the Prophet but he did not hear their petition of one hundred and fifty letters. Imam al-Husayn sent his cousin Muslim ibn Aqeel to test the sincerity of these claims and for peace of mind.

• 311 •

# Twelve thousand

In response to the letters from Kufa, Imam al-Husayn۩ made intention to go to Kufa. But before that, he sent his cousin Muslim ibn Aqeel on a fact finding mission to see if the Kufans were genuine in their claims. If they swore allegiance (*Bay'a*) and showed genuine sympathy for Imam al-Husayn and disgust at Yazid, then he could safely assume that it was okay for Imam al-Husayn to come. Imam Muslim with his two sons Muhammad and Ibrahim set off for Kufa for this mission. They reached Kufa and were greeted with a great reception. Imam Muslim stayed as the guest of Mukhtar ibn Abi Ubayd. As word spread that Imam Muslim had come, people in their hundreds came and swore allegiance to Imam Muslim. More than twelve thousand people swore allegiance to him. Imam Muslim pleased by the welcome and response of the Kufans sent a message to Imam al-Husayn in Makkah that the people of Kufa were genuine in their claims and that it was safe for him to come.

*Sirrul Shahadatayn, Saniha e Karbala*

The objective of the Ahl al-Bayt was that as servants of Allah they followed no other path but Islam. They resisted anything that was against the Shariah. They proclaimed loudly the truth. This has been and always will be the way of the people of truth.

# The tyrant ibn Ziyad

Imam Muslim was greeted in Kufa by twelve thousand people who swore an oath of allegiance straight away. Seeing this strength of commitment on the part of the Kufans, he wrote to his cousin Sayyiduna Imam al-Husayn to come straight away. When Yazid learnt of this show of support for Imam al-Husayn, he ordered the governor of Basra Ubaidullah ibn Ziyad to go to Kufa and warn the people not to side with Imam al-Husayn, otherwise they would face dire consequences. Ibn Ziyad was a very cruel and hard-hearted person. He reached Kufa and warned the people of Kufa in a gathering the consequences of rejecting Yazid's power and siding with Imam al-Husayn. He tried to entice the people to support Yazid by means of bribery. Imam Muslim was worried by these developments in Kufa so he went to Hani ibn Urwa's house. He came as a poor traveller and sought refuge as he reminded Hani the true nature of the people of Kufa. Hani accepted Imam Muslim and emptied out a room for him and his two sons to stay in. Ibn Ziyad quickly learnt that Imam Muslim had taken refuge in Hani's house. He sent some of his troops to Hani's house who was arrested. Other sympathisers of the Ahl al-Bayt and important people of the city were also arrested.

Imam Muslim realised the situation and decided to go to the Qazi's (judge's) house who was also a true follower and lover of the Ahl al-Bayt. Imam Muslim then began to call out to the people of Kufa, the response of which was phenomenal and instant. No sooner had he started calling out to the people of Kufa, people came out of their houses and on to the streets in support of Imam Muslim and Imam al-Husayn. Forty thousand people gathered in support of Imam Muslim and marched towards the Governor's palace where Ibn Ziyad was staying and laid siege to the premises. The angry people were very close to defeating Ibn Ziyad. But he came up with a cunning plan. What he did was to force the important people of the city who he had arrested before, to climb the roof of the besieged building and warn their people not to side with Imam Muslim. The "leaders" of the city fearful of the outcome in either scenario decided to do what the hard-hearted ibn Ziyad wanted. They climbed the roof of the premises and said, "O People! Your support for Imam Muslim is dangerous. The (new) government will be bad for you. Yazid will hunt down and kill your children. He will take away all your wealth and belongings. Your homes will be taken away from you. If you side with Imam Muslim, then ibn Ziyad's men will kill every Kufan in this place. Think about your position and be merciful on ours. Go to your homes now." This plea instigated by Ibn Ziyad worked. The people who came out in support of Imam Muslim turned out to be faithless and gutless. They all left Imam Muslim to fend for himself. They turned out to be so gutless that by sunset Imam Muslim was left all alone to fend for himself with his two young sons Muhammad and Ibrahim.

*Sirrul Shahadatayn, Saniha e Karbala, Tazkirah al-Husayn*

---

The people of Kufa claimed to be ardent lovers of Imam al-Husayn and the Ahl al-Bayt but turned out to be treacherous instead. We learn from this that not every claimant to be a lover of Ahl al-Bayt is true.

• 313 •

# The martyrdom of Imam Muslim

Imam Muslim went to Kufa where the Kufans swore allegiance to him and Imam al-Husayn. But under threat from Yazid, the Kufans showed their treachery in abandoning him to fend for himself.

It was night when Ibn Ziyad made an announcement for people to capture him. Imam Muslim, tired and hungry stayed inside the mosque. Imam Muslim left the mosque, not knowing where he would go next. In his mind he was thinking about Imam al-Husayn who had been told to come to Kufa. He was trying to think of a way to get a message to him not to come to Kufa. Walking around, lost in these thoughts and worries, he passed by a house. There he saw an old woman named Towha. He asked for water, which she gave to him. She found out that this was the homeless Imam Muslim. She gave a place for him to rest in her house. The woman's son was an Ibn Ziyad supporter. He went and told Ibn Ziyad that Imam Muslim was staying in his house. Ibn Ziyad and his troops surrounded the house. Imam Muslim realised that the house was under siege and with his sword fought like a lion against the enemies. He wounded several Kufan troops and killed some too. Some troops from the rooftops showered him with stones. A stone struck his forehead that caused some bleeding. Imam Muslim turned his face towards Makkah and called out, "O al-Husayn take note of the state of your brother Muslim! Look and see what the treacherous Kufans have done to me, what a shame nobody is here who can tell you about my state!" The Kufans continued to pelt poor Imam Muslim with stones. One stone hit him on the lip that spurted out with blood. His beard became coloured with blood. Imam Muslim lent back against a wall battered and bruised. A Kufan came and struck him with a sword that ripped into his lip. But Imam Muslim killed him. Imam Muslim again leaned against a wall and said, "O Allah! I am thirsty." Towha the kind lady heard his call and ran to his aide with water. As he tried to drink the water it would turn into blood, such was the viscous cut on his lips. Towha tried again to give him water but it was no use. So severe were the cuts in his mouth that his teeth fell out. In that time somebody from behind him came and struck him in the back with a spear. Imam Muslim tried to crawl away from the attacks but the oppressors got hold of him and took him to Ibn Ziyad. Ibn Ziyad ordered them to take him on to the rooftop and to execute him in front of everyone. A person by the name Ibn Bakeer took Imam Muslim on to the rooftop. As he was being lead to his death Imam Muslim was praying Salutations (*Durud*) upon the

Prophet and said, "O Allah judge with Truth (Haqq) between me and these people." All the people of Kufa had gathered down below. Imam Muslim saw them and said, "O Kufans! When my head is separated from my body, bury my body. And take my clothes and send it with a convoy on the way to Makkah and give it to Imam al-Husaynﷺ. Be merciful on my innocent children." Imam Muslim turned his face towards Qibla and said, "*Assalamo Alayka Ya Ibne Rasoolallah.*" They then executed Imam Muslimﷺ.

From Allah we have come and to Him is our return.

Tazkirah al-Husayn

---

The people drunk in worldly desires and motives killed Imam Muslimﷺ for no reason. The people of Kufa showed their true colours and acted treacherously and allowed the murder of Imam Muslim.

• 314 •

# Oppressed Children

When Imam Muslimﷺ left Makkah for Kufa, he took with him his two beloved sons. His two sons were called Sayyiduna Muhammad and Ibrahimﷺ. Ibn Ziyad having killed Imam Muslim learnt that his two sons were also in the city. Ibn Ziyad made an announcement that whoever contemplated giving refugee to the two children should think again, as they would be killed. Muhammad and Ibrahim were staying at the Judge's house. The Judge called the two children over, as he wanted to tell them something important. But as they drew near he started crying. The two boys asked the Judge why he was crying? "Have we become orphaned today?" The Judge stopped crying and said with deep breaths and said, "May Allah bless you with patience, yes, you have been orphaned." The two boys heard this dreadful news and started to cry. The Judge tried to console the boys but it was pointless, as he was heartbroken at what had tragically happened. He tried to stop the boys from crying and screaming too much as he told the boys that Ibn Ziyad's men were after them as well. The Judge told the boys of his plan to send them somehow on the next convoy to al-Madina. The boys were consoled by this and stopped crying.

The Judge told his son Asad, to look at the gate of Iraq and to see when the next convoy travels southwards to al-Madina. It was Asad's duty to get a reliable man to put the boys on the next convoy going to the City of the Prophet. When Asad took the two boys with him to the gate of Iraq, the convoy had already set off. Asad told the two boys that the convoy they see passing by is going to al-Madina and told them to run after it. The boys had no option but to run after the convoy in the hope that they caught up with it. The boys ran as fast as they could but failed to reach the caravans. Asad returned home thinking that his work had been done.

It was the middle of the night, and the two boys were lost, hungry and homeless and with enemies after their blood. They spent the night walking aimlessly around the outskirts of Kufa. It was approaching dawn, when Muhammad and Ibrahim spotted a light appear from a house. They saw a woman come and fetch some water. She saw them and asked who they were? When she learnt that they were the oppressed sons of Imam Muslim, she started crying and consoled the boys. She then took them inside. The lady of that house was a true lover of the Ahl al-Bayt. The woman helper came home and told her master that she had with her the two children of Imam Muslim. The lady of the house came running and embraced the children as if they were her own. The women then fed the starving children, and then put them to sleep in one of their rooms.

The lady of the house was a lover of Ahl al-Bayt but her husband could not have been any different. Her husband was named Haris, a greedy worldly person who had animosity for the Ahl al-Bayt. He had spent the entire day in search of the children of Imam Muslim so that he could get the reward promised by Ibn Ziyad. It was in these strange and bizarre circumstances that Haris, his wife and the two boys found themselves all under the same roof.

The lady of the house knowing the tyrant her husband was, decided to put Muhammad and Ibrahim to sleep quickly, lest her cruel husband found out and did something awful to the innocent children.

A good part of the night passed, when the elder brother woke up the younger brother so that he could say something to him. What the elder brother told his younger brother was that he saw a dream in which their father was in the Holy presence of Prophet Muhammadﷺ. Their great grandfather was talking to Imam Muslim when he enquired, "O Muslim! You have come by yourself, why have you left the children with the oppressors?" Imam Muslim replied, "O Messenger of Allah! They too will be joining us by the morning." The younger brother heard this and said that he too saw the same dream. The two boys then started to cry and scream.

Their crying woke up Haris. He asked his wife where the sounds of crying and screaming were coming from? The lady kept quiet in fear of what Haris might do to the young boys. Haris got up, and lit a lantern and entered the room in which Muhammad and Ibrahim were crying. He saw them and asked them who they were? The two boys said without hesitation that they were the sons of Imam Muslim. The tyrant Haris became happy as he heard this. For him, his dream had come true. He could now look forward to gaining the reward promised by Ibn Ziyad. Haris advanced towards the children and treated them badly as he pulled at their arms and slapped them. He tied the two boys up, as his wife tried her best to stop her husband from doing any more harm to the children. But Haris would hear none of the appeals made by his wife as his greedy mind set eyes on a reward from Ibn Ziyad. The tyrant Haris took the boys to the banks of the Euphrates, as he was about to slay them. When they saw that they were about to be murdered, the elder brother pleaded to Haris that his head be chopped off first, as he could not bear to see his younger brother being put to the sword first. The tyrant Haris picked up his sword, as the boys pleaded one final time for them to be spared, as they were orphaned and homeless. But again Haris heard none of it. He did as the elder brother requested and killed him first, and then killed the younger brother.

From Allah we have come and to Him is our return.

*Tazkirah al-Husayn*

---

Allah the Almighty says in the Qur'an that He tests His beloved followers with trials and tribulations of wealth, of children and of their own lives. And when we reflect on this episode with what happened to Imam Muslim and his two innocent children, we see that this account is the *tafsir* of this verse. The people of Allah endure these tests and trials with patience and thanks to Allah. They endure these trials with no complaints as they have already surrendered themselves to the will of Allah.

• 315 •

# Oppressor's fate

Having killed Muhammad and Ibrahim, the sons of Imam Muslim, Haris took their heads to Ibn Ziyad to claim the prize he had promised for their capture. When he arrived Ibn Ziyad saw the two young heads and asked Haris who they were? Haris told him that they were the heads of Imam Muslim's sons- Muhammad and Ibrahim. Ibn Ziyad instead of being happy was extremely angry with Haris. "What have you done you wretch? I have told Yazid that I will hand over Imam Muslim's two sons over to him alive. Why did you kill them?" Haris said, "If I brought them alive somebody may have seen them and snatched the children off me and claimed the prize instead." Ibn Ziyad said, "If you had told me then I would have met you in person or sent somebody over to receive them." Haris fell silent, as he could say no more to Ibn Ziyad who was seething with rage.

Ibn Ziyad was visibly infuriated by Haris's actions. He looked towards his men and chose a man who just so happened to be a true believer and lover of Ahl al-Bayt. Ibn Ziyad told that person to take Haris to the riverbank and kill him and to throw his body into the river. He was also told to take the two heads of Muhammad and Ibrahim and to place them in the river. This person became ecstatic at being chosen to exact revenge on the foolish Haris. He was so happy that he said to Ibn Ziyad that if he offered him the whole Islamic Caliphate he wouldn't be as pleased as he was in exacting revenge on Haris. He took Haris and tied his hands behind his back and took his turban off so his head was bare. As he passed through the streets of Kufa the people sent curses on Haris and expressed sorrow upon seeing the heads of Imam Muslims' two innocent sons. On reaching the Euphrates riverbank, he first laid to rest the heads on the river. The bodies of Muhammad and Ibrahim miraculously rose to the top of the river where their heads were joined up with their bodies. The bodies then sunk back down into the river. Haris then got what he deserved and was executed on the riverbank. The executioner slung his body into the river but within a matter of moments the river tossed his ugly and vile body out and back on the riverbank. They then tried to bury him in the ground but the earth too didn't accept his body. They collected some wood and burnt his body.

*Tazkirah al-Husayn*

---

The people who distance themselves from the deen of Islam and are treacherous in their every action deserve what they get in this world. These people are losers in this world and certain losers in the hereafter.

• 316 •

# The journey to Kufa

The day Imam Muslim was tragically killed was the same day Sayyiduna Imam al-Husayn set off from Makkah towards Kufa. He with his family and servants (82 people in all) set off on this journey northwards. They left the holy city of Makkah as young and old bid them a tearful farewell. Imam al-Husayn's convoy reached a place called Shaqooq and stopped there for a while. It was there that they met a person who told al-Husayn ibn Ali that the Kufans had betrayed his beloved cousin Imam Muslim and that he had been savagely murdered. Imam al-Husayn heard this news and said, "From Allah we have come and to Him is our return."

Imam al-Husayn then entered the tent of the convoy where his family was assembled. He went towards the daughter of Imam Muslim and gave her love as given to an orphaned child and started to talk differently towards her. The daughter noted this and asked Imam al-Husayn why he was treating her differently. "Maybe my father has been killed," she said to herself. Imam al-Husayn burst out crying and said, "O daughter! Don't fear. From now on I am your father and my wife is your mother and my sons and daughters are your brothers and sisters." The daughter of Imam Muslim began to weep. Another child of Imam Muslim learnt of their father's demise and wept. They then got up and said, "O al-Husayn! Insha Allah we will get the revenge for our father's death from the people of Kufa or we also will be martyred in Allah's way."

Imam al-Husayn got up and addressed his people. He said, "The people of Kufa have proven to be faithless and killed Imam Muslim. Whoever wishes to leave can leave." Hence some people who came along left, leaving behind only those people who were to taste the divine cup of martyrdom. They travelled on northwards until they reached a place called Shilbaa. Imam al-Husayn ibn Ali rested on his sister's (Sayyida Zaynab) lap. After a while he woke from his sleep with tears in his eyes. He said to Zaynab, "I have just seen our dear grandfather in my dream in which he was saying to me as he was crying that, "O al-Husayn! Come and meet us quickly", and one traveller is saying that the people have gone, and that death is coming our way. Sayyiduna Ali Akbar said, "O father! Are we not on the path of Truth (*Haqq*)?" Imam al-Husayn said, "Yes indeed we are and *Haqq* is on our side." Ali Akbar said, "Then why should we fear death. After all we are to die one day. O father! The garden of martyrdom is in front of us. It is infinitely better than the world."

*Tazkirah al-Husayn*

---

Sayyiduna Imam al-Husayn and his family were always in a state of readiness when it came to speaking out the words of Truth. They did not fear death at all, but in actual fact welcomed it. They also set off in defiance of Yazid's antics to Kufa knowing very well the tough times ahead of them.

• 317 •

# Hurr ibn Yazid

When Ibn Ziyad learnt that Imam al-Husayn had set off for Kufa, he sent Hurr with a taskforce of 1000 troops to stop him in his tracks. As Imam al-Husayn and his family neared Kufa they saw the taskforce come their way. He sent a person to go and see what type of army was approaching them. Within that time Hurr turned up and met face to face with Imam al-Husayn. Hurr said, "I have been sent by Ibn Ziyad to take you to Kufa." Imam al-Husayn told Hurr and his troops, "O people! It wasn't my intention to come here to Kufa. What called me here were the letters of invitation written by you people. Now that I am here you should allow me to enter Kufa as I please or let me return to where I have come from." Hurr said, "By God! We have no knowledge of any such letters." Imam al-Husayn replied, "But there are many people standing behind you who sent these letters to me." Imam al-Husaynﷺ took those letters and began to read them out. Many of the soldiers behind Hurr hung their heads. Hurr agreed to help Imam al-Husayn by telling him that he would allow him to go free once night had fell and the troops had fallen asleep. Hurr told Imam al-Husayn that in the morning he would pretend to search for him and report back to Ibn Ziyad empty handed.

*Sirrul Shahadatayn, Tazkirah al-Husayn*

---

Imam al-Husaynﷺ went to Kufa on the invitation of its people on purely religious and moral grounds. So whoever claims that he went there to build up political support for claims of the Caliphate are utterly wrong. This is because someone travelling to build up political support to overthrow a regime wouldn't do so without military assistance and they certainly wouldn't do so with their families. Imam al-Husayn set off for Kufa to live there not to conquer it.

• 318 •

# The plain of Karbala

Having found out that Sayyiduna Imam al-Husaynﷺ was on his way to Kufa, Ibn Ziyad ordered Hurr to meet Imam al-Husaynﷺ and to prevent him from going any further. When Hurr met Imam al-Husaynﷺ he suggested to him that he should camp here for the night and separate from the women for the sake of the women on the journey. Imam al-Husaynﷺ did as requested and slept with the other men. When the Yazidi forces had gone to sleep, Imam al-Husayn ﷺ woke up and left the camp. In the darkest part of the night, Imam al-Husayn ﷺ did not know where he was going or where he was. In the morning, he saw a plain where blood was coming out of the ground. From whichever tree branch he snapped blood would come out. Imam al-Husayn ﷺ turned to his people and asked, "Who can tell me the name of this plain?" One person said that this place is called Mariya. Imam al-Husayn ﷺ said, "Maybe there is another name to this place." The people then said to him that this place is called Karbala. Imam al-Husayn ﷺ heard this and said, "Allahu Akbar. This is Karbala. Our blood will be spilt and flow here. We will not leave this place alive." Ali Akbar said, "O father! Why have you said this?" Imam al-Husayn ﷺ replied, "O son! Your grandfather Ali Murtaza passed by this place he stopped here and rested on the lap of Imam Hasan. I was also present when my father woke up with tears in his eyes. Imam Hasan al-Mujtaba asked father what the matter was? Your grandfather replied, "I have just seen Imam al-Husayn ﷺ drown in a river of blood, having been beaten and hurt, calling out for help. But nobody responds to his plea." Mawla Ali then looked at me and said "O son! When you reach this place what will you do?" I said that I would exercise patience. Father in response said to me to be patient, as patience has a great reward." Imam al-Husayn ﷺ ordered the people to decamp at the banks of the Euphrates. The day Imam al-Husayn ﷺ camped at Karbala was the 2nd of Muharram in the sixty-first year after Hijrah.

*Tazkirah al-Husayn*

---

The plain of Karbala was the site of Imam al-Husayn's examination. He knew very well that he was to sit this test and it is to his credit that he made every single possible preparation for this test of patience and endurance.

・ 319 ・

# Instruction in patience

When Sayyiduna Imam al-Husayn🕊 and his family arrived in Karbala he spoke to his family members with the following words:

"Be patient in my troubles and when I am separated from you. When I am martyred do not scream and pull your hair. O Zaynab! You are the daughter of Fatima Zahra🕊. You must be patient just as our mother was when she was separated from the Messenger of Allah🕊."

*Anaratul Basair*

---

All the scholars and historians of Islam are unanimous in their opinion that Imam al-Husayn🕊 exercised patience and instructed his family members to the same all the way through this ordeal. Hence we too should live our lives with patience and gratitude to Allah Almighty, and avoid being ungrateful and impatient. By following the way and example of Ahle al-Bayt we will gain peace and comfort in our lives.

・ 320 ・

# Ibn Ziyad's letter

When Imam al-Husayn arrived in Karbala, Ibn Ziyad sent a letter to him in which he said that he must swear allegiance to Yazid otherwise he must prepare to fight. When Imam al-Husayn got this letter he threw it away, and told the person who brought the letter, that he had no reply to his ultimatum.

Ibn Ziyad heard of Imam al-Husayn's defiance and became angry. He called upon Ibn Sa'd, who for a long time had ambitions of becoming a governor of the Islamic Empire. Ibn Sa'd was told by Ibn Ziyad to go and force Imam al-Husaynﷺ into submission by all means possible otherwise he must face the consequences. He was told to chop his head off if necessary to achieve the desired result. If he did that then he would be awarded governorship, as he desired. Ibn Sa'd's greed for glory led him to take a force to Karbala to challenge Imam al-Husaynﷺ.

When Ibn Sa'd got there and met Imam al-Husayn he asked him what brought him here? Imam al-Husaynﷺ replied that the dozens of letters written by the people of Kufa brought him to Iraq. He said that he did not come on his own accord but was invited but since he learnt that they had become faithless, he wished to leave without resistance. Ibn Sa'd returned to Ibn Ziyad with Imam al-Husayn's words. Ibn Ziyad became angry with Ibn Sa'd and told him that he was not sent to compromise with him but to force him to accept their demands unconditionally. "We accept nothing but adherence to Yazid as the condition of Imam al-Husayn's freedom." Ibn Ziyad then sent the likes of Shimar and Kohli to go and pressurise Imam al-Husaynﷺ into submission to Yazid's will. Forces were sent with the order to shut off the supplies of water from the River Euphrates for Imam al-Husaynﷺ and his family.

*Tanqih-e-Shahadatayn*

---

Imam al-Husaynﷺ and his family entered the plain of Karbala for the sake of Islam. While Ibn Ziyad, Ibn Sa'd and the other tyrants entered it with worldly intentions. We learn that even when Imam al-Husayn reached Karbala he spoke and acted with complete and clear arguments. He also said that if they had no objection then he would quietly go back to where he came, but they didn't allow him to do that. The men bribed by Yazid and not Imam al-Husayn were the cause of the conflict.

# River Euphrates

Imam al-Husayn☬ and his family had set up their camp on the banks of the River Euphrates. But on the seventh of Muharram, Ibn Sa'd and his 80,000 troops came and ordered them to decamp and move away from the riverbank. Ibn Sa'd's men then prevented any more water from getting to them. Troops were lined up along the river to stop them. Among the troops that stood along the banks of the Euphrates were people who wrote letters of invitation to the grandson of the Prophet and people who claimed allegiance to him and Mawla Ali (may Allah be pleased with him). Abbas tried to dispute with Ibn Sa'd about his actions but Imam al-Husayn☬ prevented a duel between them and consoled him. Imam al-Husayn☬ told Abbas that it was wrong and futile to fight over the Euphrates, a river of the mortal world, when they had permanent access to the Pool of Kawthar belonging to the Prophet☬.

*Tanqih-e-Shahadatayn*

Imam al-Husayn's decision to move away from the riverbank as ordered by Ibn Sa'd epitomises his resolve, patience and gratitude to Allah about the whole ordeal he was being put through. He realised his mission in Karbala and it wasn't to fight over access of the Euphrates.

# Well

# Well

The Yazidis stopped water supplies reaching the camp of Imam al-Husaynﷸ from the seventh of Muharram. On the eight, when each and every member was thirsty and in search for water and when the words "water, water" were on everyone's dry lips, Imam al-Husaynﷸ dug a well from which some members of the family drank. But after a short while, the well dried out and disappeared.

*Tanqih-e-Shahadatayn*

We learn from this that Allah Almighty Himself caused the well to dry so that the test of patience and endurance, which had to be taken by Imam al-Husayn and his family, was taken under extreme and tough conditions. For Imam al-Husayn and his family the fountain of Kawthar was awaiting for them so that they could quench their thirst there for eternity.

# Bareed Hamdani and Ibn Sa'd

On the ninth of Muharram, Bareed Hamdani who was in the Husayni camp sought Imam al-Husayn's permission to go and talk to Ibn Sa'd. Ibn Sa'd said, "O Hamdani! Don't you consider me as a Muslim as you failed to say salaam to me?" Hamdani said, "What sort of claim to faith do you have when you stop water from the Euphrates reaching the Ahl al-Bayt? Animals and birds are drinking water from it but you deny the noble family of the Prophet who possess the eternal Kawthar fountain of the Hereafter? Ibn Sa'd replied, "What you say is true but what can I do, I have to follow the orders of Yazid."

*Tanqih-e-Shahadatayn*

---

The people who only have considerations for this world are totally blind to the eternal suffering and punishment of the Hereafter.

• 324 •

## Oppressed Sayyid

Imam al-Husayn⁣ﷺ spent the morning of the ninth of Muharram in talks with Ibn Sa'd. This lasted until the afternoon. After Zuhr prayer, Imam al-Husayn was sitting outside his camp reciting the glorious words of the noble Qur'an. He did so with tears runing down his cheeks. Imam al-Husayn saw a god-fearing traveller go past in the desert. Imam al-Husayn in this state told the person about his condition. "I am a traveller far from his home, being oppressed and made hungry and thirsty for no reason. The people of Kufa had invited me by sending letters of complaints and promises of support. But now they have turned their backs on me and have proved to be faithless and are now after my blood."

*Tanqih-e-Shahadatayn*

---

This message will continue to call out to Imam al-Husayn till the Day of Judgement that the people of Kufa proclaimed a love that turned out to be false and that they treated Imam al-Husayn oppressively.

# Meeting with the Prophet ﷺ

On the night of the tenth of Muharram 61 AH Imam al-Husayn ؑ was busy in the worship of Allah. In the last part of the night tiredness overtook him as he fell asleep. In his dream he saw the master of both worlds Prophet Muhammad ﷺ with a group of angels. The Prophet of Allah took Imam al-Husayn and embraced him and comforted him just like when he was a little child. The Prophet said to him, "O my Life! O coolness of my eyes! O my al-Husayn! I know very well what your enemies are up to and what they want from you. O son! Spend this remaining time in patience and gratitude to Allah. This is because all those people with your blood on their hands will be deprived of my intercession on the Day of Judgement. And on that Day you will be crowned with the great reward of *Shahadat*. In a short while you will be relieved from the rigours of Karbala. O son! Jannat has been prepared for you. Your mother and father are waiting at the gates of Jannat." The Prophet then embraced Imam al-Husayn ؑ and did dua for him and said, "O Allah give my al-Husayn patience and reward." Imam al-Husayn ؑ woke up from this dream and told his family about it. After he spoke they all began to look at each other.

*Tanqih-e-Shahadatayn*

---

The Prophet of Allah was a witness (Shahid) of the events of Karbala. He was witnessing his grandson's patience and perseverance and he was witnessing the oppressor's oppression and tyranny.

# Threat

On the tenth of Muharram, Imam al-Husayn﷽ dug a trench around the tents of the Ahl al-Bayt to protect them from the enemy. He gathered dry wood and sticks and put them into the trench and set them on fire. An enemy saw this and said, "O al-Husayn! You have surrounded yourself in fire before the fire of Hell" (Ma'azallah, Allah forbid). Imam replied, "O enemy of Allah! You have lied." Imam al-Husayn ibn Ali then faced towards the Qibla and said, "O Allah! Drag and pull him towards the fire." No sooner had he finished the dua the enemy fell of his horse. The reins of the horse fell out of his hands and got wrapped round his feet. The horse got up again and started running and tossed the man into the fire and went away. Imam al-Husayn﷽ prostrated in thanks to Allah. He raised his head and said, "O Allah! We are the family of your Messenger. Deliver us justice from our oppressors." Another enemy of Islam appeared and said to Imam, "Do you see the Euphrates? Look how much enjoyment we are getting from it. But for you there is not even one drop of water from it and this is the state you will die in." Imam heard this and called out, "O Allah! Kill him a thirsty man." No sooner had Imam uttered these words the man fall of his horse. The man got up and went chasing after his stray horse. The man felt thirsty and began to call out for water but no one heard him and the man died of thirst.

*Tazkirah al-Husayn*

---

Sayyiduna Imam al-Husayn﷽ is a beloved of Allah. He loves Allah and Allah loves him hence the meaning of *Radi Allah Anhu*. Whatever Imam al-Husayn wanted Allah would grant straight away. But at Karbala this would not always be the case because Karbala was his examination room, and no extra help would be allowed. The story of Karbala had been written on the Preserved Tablet and could not be changed. It was the wish of Allah that Imam al-Husayn sat this stern test of patience and endurance as a lesson for us all and so he could earn the title of Sayyidus Shuhada- the leader of martyrs.

• 327 •

# Peace of mind

The Yazidi forces were in no mood to listen to compromises and wanted conflict with Imam al-Husayn﷽ unless he pledged allegiance to Yazid. Imam al-Husayn dressed himself with the turban of the Prophet and the Zulfiqaar sword in his hand and rode on his camel towards Ibn Sa'd and his troops. Imam al-Husayn﷽ said, "O Iraqi's! You all know very well that I am the grandson of the Holy Prophet of Allah﷽. I am the son of Fatima Zahraa and Mawla Ali. And I am the brother of Hasan al-Mujtaba﷽. Look and see whose turban I am wearing? Don't you reflect on how even the Christians and Jews honour their Prophets? All religions revere and respect their Prophets and their families and take them as friends. I am the grandson of the Nabi Allah﷽. I am the son of the Lion of Allah (*Asadullah*). Why do you want to kill me? Why are you keeping my family thirsty for three days? Have I spilt somebody's blood or have I taken away somebody's right? You people have called me here and this is how you treat me. Think for one moment about what you are doing." Imam al-Husayn﷽ was giving this speech when cries could be heard from his camp. He told the people inside to stop crying and be patient and grateful to Allah. Imam al-Husayn told Ali Akbar and Abbas to console the family and to stop them from crying. "O Kufans! You are well aware of my noble lineage of which there is no likeness in the entire world. So think carefully about why after inviting me here with your tearful letters and pleas you now treat me so badly. Look at these letters." Imam al-Husayn once again showed them the letters but these treacherous people denied all knowledge of them. Imam al-Husayn saw their lies and deceits and excuses and was now content that he had said all that could be said to them. He had gained peace of mind and was prepared for his fate.

*Tazkirah al-Husayn*

---

Imam al-Husayn hoped that by talking directly to the Kufans they would come to their senses and realise what blunders they were embarking on. But these treacherous people could not see the light from the dark and were stubborn in their claims. Imam al-Husayn made clear of his disgust at their treatment of him and his family.

• 328 •

# Hurr

Hurr realised the unfolding situation in Karbala and joined Imam al-Husayn and his family. He initially came to Karbala to fight with Ibn Sa'd but his fate was such that he would now fight for the family of the Prophet and for the sake of Allah alone. The enemies had slaughtered the friends and well-wishers of Ahl al-Bayt. Imam al-Husayn had his family members left to fight against the forces of tyranny. Seeing this dire situation Imam called out, "Is there anyone who hears my call and will help me?" These heartfelt words entered the ears of Hurr who was at this time on the side of Ibn Sa'd. Hurr got up straight away and left the pits of Hell for the gardens of Paradise. He crossed the plain of Karbala to join that small group that had been hungry and thirsty for three days. Hurr entered the camp of al-Husayn and fell on his knees. He kissed Imam al-Husayn and sought his forgiveness and permission to fight. Imam al-Husayn forgave Hurr and gave him his blessings to become a martyr and a dweller in Paradise.

*Tazkirah al-Husayn*

When a person's fate is good then sooner or later they leave the path of error and join the path of guidance and salvation.

• 329 •

# Hurr's martyrdom

Hurr was fortunate to see sense and embrace the Husayni camp and distance himself from the Yazidis. Hurr was a very courageous fighter. While he was with Ibn Sa'd he was one of their commanders. Ibn Sa'd was very worried to see such a strong military character change sides. Ibn Sa'd sent Safwan to see if he could talk some sense into Hurr otherwise he was ordered to kill him.

Safwan went to Hurr and said, "Why has a brave and intelligent commander like you joined Imam al-Husayn when all the power lies with Yazid?" Hurr told Safwan that he could never go back. Safwan asked why to which Hurr replied, "Safwan! Yazid is impure while al-Husayn is pure and the darling of Muhammad Mustafa!" Safwan was angered and struck Hurr in the chest with his spear. Hurr broke his spear and then stabbed Safwan in such a way that killed him instantly and sent him straight to Hell. Safwan's brother saw what happened and ran straight towards Hurr. But Hurr saw the end of him too. Hurr then respectfully turned towards Imam al-Husayn and said, "Are you pleased with me?" Imam al-Husayn said that he was pleased. Imam al-Husayn said, "You are as free as your mother named you." (Hurr in Arabic means free). Hurr heard these words of encouragement and re-entered the battlefield. In the duel with a Yazidi a spear struck Hurr's horse that injured the animal. Hurr fell of his horse and started to fight on his feet. Imam al-Husayn saw this and sent for a horse to aid Hurr. Hurr got on board the horse and continued to battle away against the successive attacks of the Kufans. Hurr wished to return to Imam al-Husayn one last time but an unknown voice said to him, "Tthe women of Paradise (Houri) are waiting for you." Hurr called out, "O grandson of the Prophet! I am going towards the master of both worlds, is there any message you want me to pass on?" Imam al-Husayn cried out, "I am right behind you, I will be coming soon." Hurr valiantly fought the Yazidis until the attacks became too much for him. Hurr laid bruised and battered on the battlefield as he called out to Imam al-Husayn. Imam al-Husayn ran towards him and carried him back to the camp. He rested Hurr's head on his lap and wiped the blood and dirt of his face. Hurr opened his eyes and smiled at his leader as his soul left his wounded body. Hurr tasted martyrdom and was amongst the righteous.

From Allah we come and to Him is our return.

*Tazkirah al-Husayn; Sirre-Shahadatayn*

---

Hurr⚜ according to his name really did free himself from Hell by joining Imam al-Husayn and his family in this battle between good and evil. Hurr's Shahadat teaches us a valuable lesson that the world is for a few days and that we are to die one day and return to the Lord who created us all. So why not leave this world in such a way that Allah and His Prophet are happy with us? We should strive to adopt the traits of Hurr⚜ and the Ahl al-Bayt and avoid the way of the treacherous and hypocrites.

• 330 •

# Two lions

Sayyiduna Aoun and Sayyiduna Muhammad sought permission from their mother Sayyida Zaynab and Uncle Imam al-Husayn to fight and taste the divine cup of *Shahadat*. They left for the battlefield chanting "Allahu Akbar!" as loud as they could. These two lions of Ahl al-Bayt entered enemy lines and fought valiantly by sending some Yazidis straight to the Hell fire. When the enemy saw that these two youngsters were making inroads into their defences, they plotted to separate and isolate them from each other. The enemy soldiers were scared of fighting them. Eventually someone had the courage to challenge them as one person struck them from behind sending Sayyida Zaynab's star tumbling to the ground. The other brother was also struck to the ground as they bled to death. Imam al-Husayn﴾ saw this and ran on to the battlefield to see his two brave nephews. As Imam al-Husayn approached the two brothers opened their eyes and smiled. They then breathed their last and were now in the gardens of Paradise with the other martyrs. Imam al-Husayn returned with their bodies. Sayyida Zaynab felt terrible at seeing her two sons being killed. But she had no sorrow at all for the faithless Kufans.

From Allah we have come and to Him is our return.

*Tanqih-e-Shahadatayn*

---

The Ahl al-Bayt demonstrated their commitment and bravery throughout the ordeal of Karbala. The desire to be slain in the way of Allah was ever present. They sacrificed all they had for the sake of Allah and His Prophet. They have taught us that we too should sacrifice everything we have for the sake of Allah and His Prophet and should foster such a desire that we can sacrifice our lives and livelihood for this noble cause.

• 331 •

# Arzak the wrestler

After the martyrdom of Aoun and Muhammad, Qasim son of Imam Hasan﴾

stepped out on to the battlefield. The Yazidi forces upon seeing the beauty and dignity of Qasim began to tremble in fear. No one was volunteering to fight this lion of Allah. Amongst the Kufan forces was a wrestler by the name of Arzak. The people of Syria and Egypt held him in high regard as he had the physical strength of a thousand young men. He was one of the many people Yazid had bribed into pledging allegiance to him as he earned a salary of two thousand Dirhams per year. Arzak had with him his four mature sons in battle.

Ibn Sa'd suggested to Arzak that he go into battle and deal with Qasim. Arzak regarded this as an insult to his strength and honour and decided instead to send his eldest son to deal with Qasim. Arzak's son duelled with Qasim but within moments was lying dead on the field. Arzak was angered by this and immediately sent for his second son to exact revenge. He too duelled with Qasim and he too was killed. Arzak was furious and like a madman sent his third in battle, but he was unprepared for what was to come and Qasim dealt with him as well. Arzak's fourth son also tasted the same fate. Arzak was humiliated and couldn't believe what had happened and decided to go and deal with Qasim.

Imam al-Husaynﷺ saw this amazing battle being fought by his nephew and raised his hands towards the sky and said "O my Lord! Keep Qasim's honour intact." The duel with Arzak began and Qasim managed to fend off every single attack made by the wrestler on him with his spear. Arzak's attacks struck Qasim's horse that killed it. Imam al-Husaynﷺ immediately sent for a horse for his nephew to ride on. Qasim boarded the horse and again fended off Arzak's mighty attacks. Arzak stopped attacking with his spear and took his sword out. Qasim saw this and did the same. Arzak looked at his sword and said to Qasim, "I brought this sword for one thousand Dinars and got it sharpened and made it into a fine blade. Qasim! Where has your sword come from?" Qasim replied, "Your sons' bloodstains on my sword has given me great satisfaction and comfort." Qasim slowly crept towards Arzak and said, "I have heard that you are such a great wrestler and fighter and yet you rush into the battlefield. You come to fight me when your saddle strap is slack." Arzak unconsciously lowered his head towards the saddle strap when Qasim managed to get close enough to Arzak to slay his head with one blow. The brave and courageous Qasim saw off Arzak the wrestler and his four sons.

*Tazkirah al-Husayn*

---

The Ahl al-Bayt were brave and courageous and were well equipped to fight in battles. They knew all the tactics of fighting. We should learn from this and learn the "art of war" so we too can fight just like Qasim ﷺ did.

• 332 •

# Sayyiduna Abbas ﷺ

Battles were fought in a particular manner and it is perhaps important to explain how they worked before proceeding to describe what happened in Karbala on the tenth of Muhrarram 61AH.

Battles were fought as duels. Each side would send forth a person to combat the other. It was a fight to the death. Once one was vanquished another would be sent in their place.

Imam al-Husayn had with him not just his immediate family, but also supporters and friends that journeyed from Makkah. In the nearby villages of Karbala nestled on the banks of the river Euphrates, some people learnt of this battle and joined Imam al-Husayn. These supporters of Imam al-Husayn stood up first and one by one gave their lives in the name of Islam and as martyrs were worthy of Paradise.

Sayyiduna Abbas came to the Imam and asked his permission to go on to the battlefield. "They have crossed the limit. These tyrants have killed our well-wishers and relatives and those who are left are dying of thirst. I cannot bear to see any longer these children suffer. I am going to the Euphrates to get some water for them." Imam al-Husayn prepared his brother by giving him advice and encouragement. Abbas took with him a water bag so that he could fill it so that his brother, sister and children could drink from it.

The Yazidis had four thousand troops on the bank of the Euphrates to stop the Ahl al-Bayt from getting any water. As soon as Abbas entered the enemy line they quickly surrounded him. Abbas began to address the Yazidis. "Are you people Muslim or Kafir?" They said that they were Muslim. "So since when was it the manner of Muslims to deny people water? The family of the Prophet is thirsty and you deny them water. Don't you fear the Day of Judgement and the thirst you will feel on that Day? Imam al-Husayn, the grandson of the Messenger ﷺ is thirsty, and so are his children. At least allow me to get some water for these innocent children." Abbas's appeal was of no use to these stonehearted people. Instead they decided to attack him. Abbas fought back in such a way that he killed eighty of them and sent them straight to Hell. Somehow or another Abbas reached the Euphrates. He got the water bag and filled it with water. Abbas was tempted to drink the water that he and his family had wanted for three days, but the thought of Imam al-Husayn, Zaynab and the others stopped him. Abbas got up with the water bottle and attempted to make his way back to the camp. But again the enemy's quickly encircled him. Again he fought everyone in his way as he protected the water bottle from the enemy. An enemy named Nufal came from behind and struck Abbas on the arm and hit an arrow on the water bag. His hand got cut off and the water spilt out of the water bag. At this moment, Abbas was thinking about getting the water to the mouths of his thirsty family. This thought made Abbas cry. Abbas fell to the ground and was severely wounded. He called out for Imam al-Husayn who came running towards him to see his brother covered in blood. Abbas said, "My back is broken." Abbas saw Imam al-Husayn for the last time and breathed his last. Imam al-Husayn returned to the camp with the body of Abbas.

From Allah we have come and to Him is our return.

The Yazidis were tyrants and had no thought or care to what will happen to them on the Day of Judgement. They claimed to be Muslims, but the true Muslim is one who does not forget that Judgement Day will come and is scared of it and tries to prepare for it as best as possible. The Ahl al-Bayt teaches us never to forget the hereafter, which will last forever.

• 333 •

# Ali Akbar ﷺ

One by one, the camp of Imam al-Husayn ﷺ was losing men to fight the Kufans. His three sons were Ali Akbar, Ali Awsat or better known as Imam Zain al-Abidin and Ali Asghar. Imam Zain al-Abidin was very weak and could barely stand while Ali Asghar was still suckling. Ali Akbar, the eldest son was a mature 18 year old. Imam al-Husayn ﷺ seeing that he was the only adult left to taste martyrdom prepared himself mentally and physically for battle. He began to put on the armoury ready for battle. He entered the camp and began to say his final farewell to his family. Ali Akbar saw this and fell at the feet of his father and pleaded with his father to give him permission to fight in the battle and to taste the cup of martyrdom. Ali Akbar said to his father, "I will not be able to cope seeing your body after you have been martyred. Give me permission to taste martyrdom. Imam al-Husayn replied, "O Ali Akbar! How can I possibly witness my mature son being martyred by oppressors?" But Ali Akbar ﷺ continued to persist with his father and pleaded with him to fight against the enemy. Imam al-Husayn conceded and prepared his son to go into battle. Imam al-Husayn tied the Prophet's turban and tied the armoury on him as he mounted his horse ready for battle.

Imam al-Husayn showed great patience and resolve throughout. He prepared his eldest son with his own hands to go out into battle. Imam al-Husayn and all the Ahl al-Bayt showed not even a hint of dissatisfaction at their predicament, as they knew that all of this was a test from Allah.

• 334 •

# The martyrdom of Ali Akbar

When the son of Imam al-Husayn, Ali Akbar stepped on to the battlefield, a sense of fear entered the enemy line. Ali Akbar was eighteen years old, and his looks and appearance and stature was similar to that of the Final Prophet. Ali Akbar began to call out for someone to fight against him but nobody stepped forward. Seeing that nobody was coming forward Ali Akbar himself went into enemy lines and started to fight. He returned to the camp and told his beloved father that he was feeling thirsty. With no water to give him, Imam al-Husayn gave his son the Prophet's ring to suck on so that his thirst could be quenched. Ali Akbar felt some comfort from this and returned to the heat of battle. The youthful lion put a few more enemies to death. He then again returned to his father again asking him to quench his thirst. Imam al-Husayn this time told his son that very soon he would be at the fountain of Kawthar where he can drink as he pleased. Ali Akbar heard this good news that inspired him to go back and fight. Again Ali Akbar entered the heat of the battle. The enemy surrounded him. A tyrant by the name of Ibn Numair struck him on the back with a spear, which caused him to fall of his horse. Ali Akbar called out, "O father! Take news of your son Ali Akbar!" Imam al-Husayn ran onto the battlefield in search of his beloved son. Imam took his son's head and placed it on his lap. Ali Akbar opened his sore eyes and said, "O father! Look! There is the Messenger of Allah ﷺ with two glasses of water from Kawthar. I am saying to him to give me both cups, as I am very thirsty. But the Prophet is saying that one cup is for you and the other is for your father Imam al-Husayn. He too is thirsty. He too will come and drink this cup." Ali Akbar in his father's lap died as a martyr and went straight to Paradise.

From Allah we have come and to Him is our return

Tanqih-e-Shahadatayn

---

Imam al-Husayn was tested severely on the plain of Karbala. But he managed to deal with this stern examination with great success.

• 335 •

# Orphan

With the martyrdom of Ali Akbar ﷺ Imam al-Husayn ﷺ was left all on his own. Imam Zain al-Abidin was too weak to fight and Ali Asghar was only a babe in arms. So Imam al-Husayn began to prepare for his martyrdom. He once again instructed his family to exercise patience and gratitude. He told them to do this because this was the best thing to do. He warned them against pulling at their hairs in distress or to slap their faces or to beat their chests in anguish. He told them that such actions were unacceptable. He told them that if they cried in favour of the oppressed then that was permissible. He then took his daughter Sakina in his lap and kissed and cuddled her. He then looked at Zaynab ﷺ and said, "Sister! This daughter of mine is very precious to me and is very close to me. After I have been killed look after her and cherish her as your own." Imam al-Husayn then said to his daughter, "Daughter! By tonight you will be orphaned." Sakina heard the word orphan and said, "How will this be and why?"

Imam al-Husayn with tears in his eyes comforted his darling daughter and told her that the status of the orphan is just as great as the Martyr (*Shaheed*).

*Tanqih-e-Shahadatayn*

---

We learn from this account that in times of distress and misfortune we have been ordered to act with patience and common sense. To adopt any other path is wrong and dangerous. We must keep in mind the words of advice of Imam al-Husayn. To go against this advice would be going against the way of the Ahl al-Bayt.

• 336 •

# Ali Asghar

After the sacrifice of his eldest son Ali Akbar, Imam al-Husayn himself wished to go out on the battlefield and face the Kufans. The sound of crying however came from one of the tents as he went to enquire. He went there to find that his youngest son, Ali Asghar was extremely restless due to thirst. The six-month-old baby was thirsty for three days. His dry tongue was sticking out because of the extreme thirst it was feeling. Imam al-Husayn asked his wife Sayyida Zaynab to bring Ali Asghar over. Imam al-Husayn took his six-month-old child out of the tent and went towards the oppressors. He approached them and said to them, "O people! In your eyes if anyone is a criminal then it is I. But this child has done nothing wrong. Have mercy on this innocent child and allow this travelling Sayyid to have some water from the river. O people! Whoever of you gives water to this child today, I promise them a drink of water from the fountain of Kawthar on the Day of Judgement."

Despite this heartfelt appeal by Imam al-Husayn for the sake of his six-month-old child, the Kufans remained stonehearted and even more defiant in their stance against Imam al-Husayn. One tyrant by the name of Harmil ibn Kahil threw an arrow that pierced the body of the innocent Ali Asghar. Blood spurted out from his neck as Ali Asghar was sacrificed in the arms of Imam al-Husayn. The baby died as his eyes were fixed on his father's face. Imam al-Husayn kissed his darling son as he had made his way to Jannah. Imam al-Husayn carried his youngest son as he returned to the camp and handed him over to Sayyida Zaynab and said, "Even Ali Asghar has gone and tasted the water of Kawthar." The remaining members of the Ahl al-Bayt at Karbala felt agitated and restless at the sorry sight of Ali Asghar's tiny body. Tears would not cease to flow from Imam al-Husayn's eyes.

From Allah we have come and to Him is our return.

Tazkirah al-Husayn

---

The extent of the Yazidis oppression and tyranny was typified by this account. Mercy and love for children had all but disappeared from these tyrants. So how could these people be hopeful of Allah's mercy?

• 337 •

# Shaharbano's dream

On the night of Ashura, Shaharbano, the wife of Imam al-Husayn, had a dream in which she saw a veiled holy woman looking very distressed. The lady was sweeping the plains of Karbala. She approached the veiled figure and asked, "Who are you?" The veiled lady replied, "I am Fatima Zahra daughter of the Messenger of Allah. In the morning my darling al-Husayn will be killed here. I am sweeping the ground so that no stones wound my son."

Tanqih-e-Shahadatayn

Imam al-Husayn's blessed mother Sayyida Fatima Zahra 🌺 also had knowledge of the trials and tribulations her darling son was going through. This dream was a reminder that his family had not forgotten them and that they were witnessing every single action.

· 338 ·

# Farewell

On the tenth of Muharram, on the plains of Karbala all the relatives and well-wishers had been martyred and tasted the cup of martyrdom. With no one left physically fit to fight the enemy, Imam al-Husayn 🕮 made preparations to go on to the battlefield. Imam al-Husayn changed his clothes. He wore an Egyptian long gown, the turban of the Holy Prophet, the shield of Ameer Hamza and the Zulfiqar sword of Sayyiduna Ali Murtaza. He mounted his horse with the intention to go into battle.

In this time, his remaining son, Imam Zain al-Abidin appeared in front of him. He was extremely ill and could barely stand up. But despite his illness, he said to his beloved father, "That as long as I am alive, I will not allow you to go on to the battlefield. Please give me permission so that I to can fight and taste martyrdom and so that I can go and meet my brothers." Imam al-Husayn 🕮 heard these words and started to weep and said, "O comfort of the life of al-Husayn! Go and sit in the camp of Ahl al-Bayt and don't think of *Shahadat*. The family of the Prophet will continue through you so that until the Day of Judgement there will be people with the blood of the Prophet running inside them." Imam Zain al-Abidin became quiet at these words. Imam al-Husayn then gave his beloved son advice and gave him his will and told him everything he needed to know both knowledge of the inward and outward (*Zahir* and *Batin*). He began to tell all the knowledge and secrets to his son, that knowledge he gained directly from the Messenger of Allahﷺ. Having disclosed everything he needed to Imam Zain al-Abidin, Imam al-Husayn entered the camp and prepared to say farewell to his beloved family.

Farewell O Ahl al-Bayt of Mustafa
Farewell the family of the Prophet, Farewell!

Then embracing Abid he said
O my beloved, Farewell!

Then to Zaynab and Kulthum he said
Your brother says to you, Farewell!

Then to Sakina he addressed
O my oppressed daughter, Farewell!

To Sharebano, the king said
O my comforter (in pain) Farewell!

Allah is Hafiz, O friends!
Patience, oppressed and restless one, Farewell!

*Tanqih-e-Shahadatayn*

---

Imam Zain al-Abidin in the state of extreme illness showed his enthusiasm and desire to go out and fight in the way of Allah. So what can be said of those fit and able people who cannot even pray their daily prayers? We learn that there was wisdom in the illness of Imam Zain al-Abidin as the Ahl al-Bayt was maintained through his presence after Karbala. Had he too been martyred then the family of the Prophet would not be amongst us today.

# The Lion's attack

With all his family and supporters martyred Imam al-Husaynﷺ stepped out onto the battlefield of Karbala. He began to read poetic verses that were read in battle which help arouse the martial spirit of a fighter. And for some more peace of mind he made more comments at Ibn Sa'd and the treacherous Kufans. But they were deaf to his words as their spears and swords gleamed in the blazing heat of Karbala. Imam al-Husaynﷺ with the Zulfiqaar in his hand leapt into battle with such ferocity and determination just like the lion in the jungle pounces on its prey. Imam al-Husaynﷺ made severe inroads into the Kufan defences and killed scores of them and sent panic through their camp, sending them straight to death.

*Tanqih-e-Shahadatayn*

Imam al-Husayn is the son of the 'Lion of Allah.' And like a lion in the jungle Imam al-Husayn made short work of his prey in battle and made the enemies extremely scared.

# Final meeting

When Imam al-Husayn stepped on to the battlefield, he did so with such bravery and awe that the enemies were taken in by it. A person called Ibn

Qutba came forward and said, "O al-Husayn! All your friends and family have been slaughtered, leaving you to fight. How will you fight against a thousand men? Imam al-Husayn said, "Have you come to fight me, or have I come to fight you? You have blocked my path and killed my dear ones. What else can I do at this point but fight you? Don't talk too much and come and let's fight." Imam al-Husayn then gave such a loud call that the entire enemy forces became senseless and were unwilling to challenge Imam al-Husayn. Imam al-Husayn slew the enemy and charged towards the forces that began to flee. Ibn Istaah saw this and said, "O cowards! One man is left, and you are running away. Wait and I will challenge him. He said this and came in front of Imam al-Husayn. The Yazidi tried to lift his sword, but Imam al-Husayn was too quick for him and chopped him in half and sent him straight to Hell. Imam al-Husayn then started to make his way to the Euphrates River.

Shimr saw Imam al-Husayn's move and shouted, "O army! Do not let al-Husayn anywhere near the water. If you allow him to drink from the river, then every single one of you will be killed. All of you attack him." The forces heard the words of Shimr and launched an attack on al-Husayn. Imam al-Husayn lifted his sword and butchered these cruel and heartless people to death and made severe inroads into enemy lines. In doing this, Imam al-Husayn reached the banks of the river. His horse put his head into the water to drink. Imam al-Husayn wished to drink from the river as well when the deceitful people called out and said, "O al-Husayn! You are drinking water here, while your camp is been ransacked." Imam al-Husayn spilt the water and went straight away to his camp. On the way he sent some more Yazidis to the Hell fire as they tried to stop him. Imam al-Husayn arrived to see that the enemy had played a trick on him and that nothing had happened to the camp. He then entered the camp where his family was sitting. He said to his family, "Spread the sheets, do not cry and weep bitterly, be ready and prepared for problems and keep my orphans well kept." He then embraced Imam Zain al-Abidin once more and said to him, "O son! When you arrive in al-Madina, say my salaams to the people. Tell them that when they face any difficulties then they should remember me, and when you drink water remember me." Imam al-Husayn completed his final meeting and went back on to the battlefield.

*Tazkirah al-Husayn*

---

Muslims will remember the courage, efforts, determination and perseverance of Imam al-Husayn until the Day of Judgement. The loss of his family and friends, his hunger and thirst, and the severe oppression and tyranny meted out by his evil and cruel opponents were all factors going against him. But despite this he showed great patience and endurance and thanks to Allah in this most testing of times.

• 341 •

# Imam al-Husayn's martyrdom

Sayyiduna Imam al-Husayn having met his family one last time entered the battlefield and was attacked at once by the Kufans. Imam al-Husayn was up for the challenge and fought courageously. But the repeated attacks led to severe wounds on his body. Such was the ferocity of the attacks that Imam al-Husayn's horse could barely stand. Hence Imam al-Husayn was left on the battlefield all on his own. A person advanced and attacked Imam al-Husayn with a sword. He got hold of his arm and pulled it in such a forceful manner that the Yazidis arm separated from his shoulder. All the other enemies were looking at Imam al-Husayn. He knew that they were all after his blood and that survival was virtually impossible. The enemies from far started to attack him with arrows. An arrow struck Imam al-Husayn in the forehead. As the blood spurted out from his forehead, Imam wiped the blood of his face.

Imam al-Husayn suffered seventy-two wounds on his blessed body from spears, arrows and swords. It was in this state that Imam al-Husayn turned his face towards the Qibla so that he could remember his Lord and Creator. An arrow struck Imam al-Husayn on the neck. Zar'ah ibn Shareek struck him on the hand and Shimr on the head. Sunaan ibn Anas struck him with a spear in the back. Imam al-Husayn fell off his horse having faced these repeated attacks.

The time had just passed midday and the time for Jum'ua had started. Imam al-Husayn even in his condition did not forget to praise his Lord and began to pray to the Almighty. His *Qiyaam* was on his horse, his ruku was his falling of the horse and his sajda was when he fell on to the bloody ground of Karbala. Shimr came along and sat on Imam's chest. Imam opened his blooded eyes and said, "Who are you?" "I am Shimr," replied the tyrant. Imam requested him to show his chest to him, which he did. Imam al-Husayn saw that mark on Shimr's chest that the Prophet of Allah told him about in his dream. Imam said, "My grandfather is truthful." Imam then said, "Shimr, do you know what day it is?" Shimr replied, "Yes I do, it is Friday." Imam then asked, "And what time is it?" Shimr replied it is the time for Khutba and Salaah of Jum'ua." Imam then said, "At this moment Imams are standing on the pulpit and are praising Allah and His Beloved Prophetﷺ and you are sitting on the wounded body of his beloved grandchild. Where the Prophet of Allah would embrace me and kiss me and cuddle me I am now wounded and battered. At this moment to my left is the innocent Zakariyya⸵ and to my right is the innocent Yayha⸵. Shimr! Get off my chest so I can complete my Salaah to my Lord. Do whatever you wish after that. To pray to Allah with wounds and cuts is the way of my father." Shimr got off Imam al-Husayn's chest as he turned his face again towards the Qibla and offered Salaah. It was in the state of sajda that the tyrant Shimr separated the head of Imam al-Husayn from his body and killed him. On Friday 10th Muharram 61 years after Hijrah, Imam al-Husayn ibn Ali﷜ was martyred in the plain of Karbala at the age of fifty-six.

From Allah we have come and to Him is our return.

*Tazkirah al-Husayn, Tanqih-e-Shahadatayn*

Imam al-Husayn ﷺ displayed immense amounts of patience and perseverance, as the people of Kufa were oppressing him. In every condition from al-Madina to Makkah and then on his journey towards Kufa and Karbala, we see the Imam of Martyrs having faith in Allah, always worshipping Him, always relying on Him and always being patient as his noble grandfather had told him to do. Even after suffering 72 wounds to his blessed body after being hungry and thirsty for three days and seeing all his family including his 6 month old child being brutally martyred for no reason, Imam al-Husayn did not forget Allah and we see Imam al-Husayn in sajda to his Lord as his head was separated from his body. It was in sajda, in proximity to his Lord that his life was taken away from him and he earned the status of *Sayyidus Shuhada*- leader of the Martyrs. So we Muslims should reflect on this important event and strive to pray our daily prayers on time and when possible with Jama'at. If we don't then with what face can we present ourselves to Imam al-Husayn ﷺ, whom we revere and respect, on the Day of Judgement if we fail to remember Allah? Hence we should follow the way of Imam al-Husayn ﷺ who was given this high honour and status because he gave his life and the life of his whole family in the face of a strong opposition so that the sanctity and honour of Islam- the Islam of the Prophet ﷺ and his four rightly guided caliphs ﷺ remained intact. For the sake of the Truth we should strive to defend the Truth against falsehood. And moreover we should never forget the remembrance of Allah at any time. We should remember Allah at all times even if our lives, family, wealth and property are at stake.

· 342 ·

# Umme Salama's dream

An old woman says that she saw Ummul Momineen Umm Salama ﷺ crying upon seeing a dream. I asked her the matter. She said to me that the Holy Prophet Sayyiduna Muhammad ﷺ appeared in my dream. The Prophet's face and beard was dusty and dishevelled. I asked, "O Messenger of Allah! What is the matter?" He said to me, "I have just come from Karbala. Today my al-Husayn has been martyred."

*Tirmidhi Sharif*

Sayyiduna Muhammadﷺ was a witness of the martyrdom of Imam al-Husayn﷜. The Holy Prophet himself viewed this great test that his beloved grandson had to endure. We learn from this that Allah's final Prophetﷺ is alive, and that he is aware of the actions of his Ummah, near and far.

• 343 •

# Deceit

On the 12th of Muharram, Ibn Sa'd took the remaining members of the Ahl al-Bayt as prisoners and the heads of the Shaheed and set off for Kufa. As they approached the city Ibn Ziyad learnt that they were coming. Ibn Ziyad made a crier make an announcement that no one was allowed outside their houses with weapons. He placed his troops on the streets to maintain law and order. The people of Kufa learnt that the Ahl al-Bayt were coming and started to run towards the convoy. As they saw the prisoners and the heads of the Shaheed they began to cry and weep. Imam Zain al-Abidin﷜ looked at them and said, "Why are you are crying for us when you are responsible for this?"

*Tazkirah al-Husayn*

Every person that sheds tears and weeps is not genuine, just as this incident shows. Oppressors and criminals often cry and weep in order to deflect criticism and blame for their crimes. But these actions are just pure deceit.

# Long live al-Husayn ؓ !

Zayd ibn Arqam ؓ who was a noble companion of the Prophet says that when the head of Imam al-Husayn ؓ was being taken through the streets of Kufa, he was in his apartment. When the head of al-Husayn passed near his house he heard the following ayat come from the lips of Imam al-Husayn:

> **"Do you reflect that the Companions of the cave (Ashab al-Kahf) were our wonderful signs?"**
>
> (18:9)

Hearing this gave Zayd goose pimples in astonishment. Zayd called out, "O Grandson of the Prophet! By Allah! Your story is stranger than this one being recited."

The head of Imam al-Husayn then reached Ibn Ziyad and was placed on a spear for everyone to see. The lips of Imam al-Husayn were once again moving. Everyone was anxious to hear what Imam al-Husayn was saying. When they all fell silent they heard the following words on Imam's lips:

> **"And never think that Allah is unmindful of the misdoings of these wrongdoers...**
>
> (14:42)

*Tazkirah al-Husayn*

Those who give their lives in the way of Almighty Allah do not die, but are in actual fact alive. The Qur'an states "And do not speak of those who are slain in the way of Allah as dead. Nay they are but alive only you cannot percieve it." (2:154) Imam al-Husayn؏ is not only alive as a Shaheed but he is *Sayyidus Shuhada* - the king of martyrs.

• 345 •

# Aziz ibn Harun

After staying in Kufa for a few days the Ahl al-Bayt and the heads of the Shaheed were taken to Damascus in Syria where Yazid resided. On the way to Syria the convoy stopped at a place called Halb, which was in the shadows of a mountain. On the mountainside was a small settlement. The leader of this settlement was a Jew by the name of Aziz ibn Harun. Shaharbano's slave-girl approached her master with tears and sorrow in her eyes and asked permission to buy some clothes for her with some money she had left. Shaharbano gave permission as she went up into the mountainside. The slave girl knocked on the door of a big house which Aziz ibn Harun himself opened and called out to the slave-girl by name and with great honour and respect.

Sheri the slave girl asked Aziz how he knew her name when they had only just met? Aziz ibn Harun told her that he had a dream in which Prophet Musa and Sayyiduna Harun (peace be upon them) were looking very distraught. Aziz asked them how they were when Musa and Harun replied that the Final Prophet of Allah's family was being troubled and oppressed. They informed Aziz ibn Harun that the Ahl al-Bayt of the Prophet would be made prisoners and would pass by this mountain. Aziz asked them, "Do you know the Final Prophet Muhammad؟?" They replied, "O Aziz! He is the truthful Prophet. Allah has made us take an oath on him. We believe firmly in him. Whoever denies him is destined for Hell." Aziz asked for proof of their claim when they told him to wait for a person tonight called Sheri.

They told Aziz to obey her and to accept Islam there and then. They also told Aziz to convey salaams to the head of Imam al-Husayn☀.

No sooner had Aziz woke up from this dream did Sheri knock on the door. Sheri the slave girl returned to her master Shaharbano and told her about the whole story. Upon hearing this, the Ahl al-Bayt were bemused and surprised.

In the morning Aziz ibn Harun paid a small bribe to the Yazidis keeping guard the Ahl al-Bayt as he went to meet them. He met them and gave them clothes and money. He gave Imam Zain al-Abidin one thousand Dinars. He read the Kalima and became a true believer. He then respectfully approached the head of Imam al-Husayn☀ and conveyed his personal salaams and that of Sayyiduna Musa and Sayyiduna Harun (peace be upon them).

*Tazkirah al-Husayn*

---

The blessings and legacy of Imam al-Husayn☀ continued and continues after his Shahadat. A Jew believing in Sayyiduna Musa and Harun (peace be upon them) was guided to the Truth on the instructions of the Prophet's he believed in. He was most fortunate to accept Islam at the hands of the Ahl al-Bayt. We learn that it is the Sunnah of Musa and Harun the Prophets of Allah to love and follow the Final Prophet of Allah and to love his family. We also learnt that the blessings and honour of people close to Allah continues uninterrupted after they leave the mortal world.

• 346 •

# The priest

The Yazidis were taking the captives of Karbala and the head of Imam al-Husayn to Damascus when it stopped on the way at a very strongly built church. The Yazidis wanted to stay there as night fell. Inside the church lived an old priest. Shimr spoke to the old priest and told him that they wished to stay the night. The priest asked them who they were and where they were going. Shimr told him that they were the soldiers of Ibn Ziyad, and that they were taking the head of a rebel and his captive family to Damascus. The priest then asked about the head? Shimr showed the priest the head of Imam al-Husayn ﷺ. No sooner had he done that, a sense of intense awe struck the priest. The priest began to say that there were too many of them to stay in his church. So what he suggested was that the prisoners and the head stayed inside the church while Shimr and his band of men would stay outside. Shimr thought well of the offer as the prisoners were secure. The head of Imam al-Husayn was placed in a box inside an inner apartment while the Ahl al-Bayt prisoners were put into a room. In the middle of the night, the priest saw light come from the inner apartment. The priest got up and went to see light coming from all four directions. After a while the roof of the inner apartment split open. Sayyida Khadija ﷺ and the other wives of the Prophet ﷺ with Sayyiduna Muhammad ﷺ came and opened the box and began to look at the head of Sayyiduna Imam al-Husayn. After a while a voice from nowhere said, "O old priest! Stop looking as Sayyida Fatima Zahra is coming!" The priest heard this and fell unconscious. When he came to his senses his eyes were covered but he could hear the following words being said as they cried and wept, "Assalamu Alaikum O oppressed mother! O martyred mother! Don't grieve as I will gain revenge from your enemies, and I will gain justice for you from Allah." The Priest again fell unconscious. When he came to his senses he became very eager to open the box. He broke the lock to the box and lifted the head of Imam al-Husayn. He then bathed the head in musk and rose water and placed it in front of him as he prepared to talk to it. The priest said, "O leader! I have learnt that you are the one whose praise and desciption has been given in the Torah and Bible. Be my witness that I become a Muslim." The priest read the Kalima and became a true believer.

*Tazkirah al-Husayn*

_____

On the face of it, the people of Allah leave this mortal world, but their works continue after their death. We learn that after his death, Imam al-Husayn ﷺ showed Christians the straight path by turning them into Muslims.

• 347 •

# Drum beating

As the Ahl al-Bayt convoy neared Damascus, Yazid learnt of their impending arrival and made preparations for it. He ordered for the city to be decorated and for the people to come out of their houses and to be joyous and festive. A Sahabi named Sahl ﷺ happened to be on business in Damascus at the time and enquired as to what was going on with the beating of drums and clapping. He was told that the head of Imam al-Husayn was being brought here from Iraq. The people told him that the convoy would arrive from Bab al Sa'at. Sahl quickly made his way to the road that would lead him towards the Ahl al-Bayt. He saw the Ahl al-Bayt convoy and cried in anguish at seeing the head of the Prophet's grandson on the top of a spear. The Ahl al-Bayt not knowing who he was asked the man why he was crying? Sahl ﷺ asked the person what is your name? The young Lady replied, "I am Sakina daughter of Imam al-Husayn." Sahl told her that he was a Companion of the Prophet ﷺ. Sahl requested them for an opportunity to help them. Sakina asked Sahl to move her father's head to the front of the convoy so that the people of Damascus were focussed on him and not on the veiled women of Ahl al-Bayt. Sahl ﷺ respectfully carried out Sakina's wish.

*Tazkirah al-Husayn*

---

We learn from this that it is the way of Yazid to be festive and joyous in the month of Muharram. The story clearly illustrates the amount of respect and honour the Companions of the Prophet had for his noble family ﷺ.

# Disrespect

The heads of the martyrs and the captives were taken from Karbala to Damascus. As they were about to enter Damascus, Yazid adorned the road leading to the palace and called many guests to witness the unfolding events. When they arrived, Yazid ordered that the captives be placed to one side. He ordered that the head's be brought in front of him. He began to look at each and every one of them and began to ask how the captives were. After hearing their state of affairs, Yazid would keep quiet and lower his gaze. He then ordered that the head of Imam al-Husayn be brought in front of him, which was placed on a large tray. When the head was placed on the tray and was brought to Yazid, he got a stick and started to point with it towards Imam's lips and teeth. He then said, "What, are these al-Husayn's lips and teeth?" Abu Barzah al-Aslami a noble Companion of the Holy Prophet was present at the time are said, "You are touching that part of his body with a stick which Sayyiduna Muhammad ‏ﷺ‎ used to kiss, and which I witnessed." Yazid immediately ordered the removal of the companion from the gathering.

*Tazkirah al-Husayn*

---

Yazid was an adulterer and a wicked person who was also arrogant, rude and a person who had no respect for the living or the dead. The Companions had utmost respect for the family of the Prophet and spoke the truth in front of oppressive leaders.

• 349 •

## False tears

When the Ahl al-Bayt arrived in Yazid's palace in Damascus, Yazid's wife Hinda entered his court impatiently to see what was happening. Yazid ran towards her and covered her head with a scarf and said to her, "Hinda! You are too quick to mourn over the loss of the Prophet's grandson when the accursed Ibn Ziyad was hasty in dealing with him about which I am not happy."

*Jila al Ayoun*

This was a big deceit on the part of Yazid and his family to show remorse at Imam al-Husayn's martyrdom when he was responsible for it all along.

• 350 •

## The call of Allah

Yazid surveyed the captives presented before him and enquired about Imam Zain al-Abidin. He was under the impression that he too had been slayed in Karbala but was clearly wrong. He called him forward and also called his son. He gave them a sword each and told them to duel. In that time the Yazidi anthem was played out. Yazid's son said with great pride, "Is this anthem being played in my father's honour or is it in your Lord's name?" Imam was about to give a response when straight after the Azan took place. After the Azan he said, "Look, my great grandfather's name is said in this call to prayer which will be given till the Day of Judgement, whereas your father's name will echo for a few days and that's all." Yazid and his son became speechless, as Imam Zain al-Abidin's words intrigued the other people gathered.

*Tazkirah al-Husayn; Tanqih-e-Shahadatayn*

---

The blessed names of Imam al-Husayn and the Ahl al-Bayt will be remembered untill the Day of Judgement, while there will be few if any people ready to remember and call out Yazid's name. We learn from this that tyranny leads to self-destruction and annihilation while patience and thanks to Allah leads to acceptance and recognition by the Almighty.

• 351 •

# Imam Zain al-Abidin in the Jamia Masjid of Damascus

Imam Zain al-Abidin was presented to the tyrant Yazid in his court. Yazid said to him, "O son of al-Husayn! Are there any requests I can fulfil for you?" Imam Zain al-Abidin said, "I have a wish and that is you hand over those people who killed my father." Yazid however rejected this wish. Imam then asked Yazid to hand over the head of his father so that it could be buried with its body and so that it could rest in peace. Yazid accepted this request. Yazid then asked Imam if he had any other request. Imam Zain al-Abidin asked for him and his family to be allowed to go back to their home in al-Madina. Yazid also accepted this request. Yazid again asked Imam if there was anything else he wanted fulfilling. Imam Zain al-Abidin asked Yazid to allow him to lead the Jumu'a prayer in the Jamia Masjid of

Damascus. Yazid accepted.

So the next day Imam Zain al-Abidin climbed the stairs of the pulpit for Juma Khutba. After praising Allah and His Messenger he began his sermon. The people inside the Masjid anticipated every word and action of Imam Zain al-Abidin as he sat on the pulpit.

Imam said, "Those who know who I am know and those who don't let me tell them. I am the great grandson of the Prophet of Allah, the grandchild of Mawla Ali and Sayyida Fatima. I am the nephew of Hasan al-Mujtaba and the son of Imam al-Husayn. I was kept thirsty and hungry with my family for three days in the baking heat of Karbala. My father and other men with us were all killed for no reason at all." The people inside the Masjid heard this, which caused great commotion. The reaction of the people scared Yazid who then ordered the Muezzin to stand up and give the *Iqama*. He took off his turban and threw it and the Muezzin and told him to stop for the sake of the Prophet of Allah. The Muezzin fell silent.

Imam Zain al-Abidin then said, "Yazid! Is Muhammad Mustafa my grandfather or yours? If you say he is yours then everyone including yourself knows that you lie. And if he is my grandfather then tell me, why did you kill my father without reason? You have orphaned me. You have made my family migrate and leave our home. You bring us to Karbala where you oppress us and insult us by imprisoning us. You have caused fractures in the *Deen* of Muhammad even though you read his kalima, and you have no shame." Imam Zain al-Abidin then turned towards the worshippers and said, "Are any of you related to the Prophet?" The people having finally realised what had happened in Karbala again erupted in commotion as they began to cry. Yazid told the Muezzin off and told him to complete the *Iqama*. After Jumu'a prayer Yazid called a meeting to allay the fears of the people of Damascus about what really happened. He presented the events in Karbala on the tenth of Muharram in such a way in which he blamed and humiliated the chieftains of Kufa (who he appointed and bribed) and scolded and cursed Ibn Ziyad in particular for what had happened. He cursed Ibn Ziyad and the

Kufans and made it look like that he had nothing to do with it.

*Tazkirah al-Husayn, Tanqih-e-Shahadatayn*

Yazid was a very clever and deceitful dictator. He ordered the murder of the Ahl al-Bayt and then turned round and cursed the Kufans in front of the people to make it look like that he had nothing to do with the tragedy of Karbala.

• 352 •

# The return to al-Madina

Yazid allowed the captives and the heads of the martyrs to go back to al-Madina al-Munawara. Nu'man ibn Bashir♦ was appointed as their guide from Damascus to al-Madina. Nu'man ibn Bashir treated the heads and captives with great honour and respect. The captives were relieved that such a noble man was leading them back home. They were so happy that they prayed abundantly for him. When the blessed and noble inhabitants of al-Madina learnt that the Ahl al-Bayt was returning, they all made preparations to receive them. All the people of al-Madina, young and old ran out to go and welcome the Ahl al-Bayt. When they arrived, they went directly to the Blessed Chamber and offered their heartfelt Salaams upon the master of the universe Sayyiduna Muhammad♦. The Salawat and Salaams offered by them was such that tears flowed from everyones eyes as they weeped bitterly. The Ahl al-Bayt were expressing their feelings to The Messenger of Allah♦ when Ummul Momineen Sayyida Umm Salama♦ appeared in front of them. She had with her the glass full of soil, which the Holy Prophet told his beloved wife would turn into blood the day Sayyiduna Imam al-Husayn♦ would be sacrificed. In the other hand she had a small turban. The Ahl al-Bayt saw her and the glass of soil that had turned into blood in her hands and began to feel even more agitated and restless. Agony and pain had descended upon al-Madina as everyone, young and old were very restless and were shedding tears.

*Tazkirah al-Husayn, Tanqih-e-Shahadatayn*

---

The events of Karbala are a very painful and poignant one that every true Muslim is touched by whenever they hear it. For believers there are countless lessons, admonitions and advice for those who wish to reflect. Muslims therefore should try their utmost best to follow the path of the Ahl al-Bayt, the path of truth. One should be willing to sacrfice everything to stay on this path. One should at the same time avoid the decieved and misguided path of those who avoided the way of Ahl al-Bayt.

• 353 •

# Imam Zain al-Abidin ﷺ

The surviving son of Imam al-Husayn at Karbala, Ali Awsat ibn al-Husayn was known as Zain al-Abidin because of his extreme devotion to his Lord.

Day and night he would devote himself to excessive voluntary nawafil prayers. Once he was in prayer on the rooftop when a fire broke out down below.

People rushed out to extinguish the fire but Imam Zain al-Abidin continued his prayers with utmost devotion and attention. They waited to ask him why on earth he did not break his prayer when his life was in potential danger. He replied, 'You were busy putting out the worldly fires while I was busy extinguishing the fires of the hereafter!'

*Raudhal Rayaheen, Haywatul Haiwan*

Zain al-Abidin's excessive and complete devotion to Allah in prayer did not allow him to be distracted. Yet we easily get distracted in prayer, often not knowing what we have just read and what it means. Imam Sahib is of the Ahl al-Bayt and by definition a Jannati. Yet he is keen to extinguish the Hell fire. How hard are we trying to put out the fire of the hereafter?

• 354 •

## Imam's endurance

Imam Zain al-Abidin once came across a rude man who was badmouthing him. He calmly said to the man, 'O brother! Whatever you have said, if it is true then I ask Allah to forgive me.' The rude insolent man became ashamed of his actions. He stepped forward and kissed his forehead and said, 'O ibn al-Husayn! What I said, you are not at all like that. I am a liar. Please pardon me and petition our Lord.' Imam Zain al-Abidin pardoned him.

*Raudhal Rayahaan*

The people who follow the commands of Allah and His Messenger ﷺ have such awe about them that even the rudest of people are softened by their humble and humane approach to matters. We learn that it is the way of the Ahl al-Bayt to pardon people and not to store up hostility against one another.

# Dangerous snake

The Caliph Mansur once told his minister that he wanted Imam Ja'far al-Sadiq﷽ summoned to his court so that he could be killed. The minister told Mansur that the killing of a Sayid was a very bad thing to do. Mansur became angry at the statement by his minister and told him to obey his orders. While the minister went to call Imam Ja'far, Mansur was instructing one of his servants how he wished for Imam Ja'far to be killed. Mansur planned to take off his crown as a signal, which would tell the servant to go and attack Imam Ja'far. By the time he had given the instructions to the accomplice, the minister had returned with Imam Ja'far al-Sadiq. The Imam was about to enter the door, when Mansur ran towards the door to greet his guest. He took him and sat him down on his seat and sat down in front of him like a lover looks into his darling's eyes. The slave ordered to carry out the attack was dumbstruck by what he was seeing as he believed that the plan was to kill him and not greet and welcome him. Mansur went out of his way to serve and be hospitable towards him. Imam Ja'far responded that in future, he wished that he wasn't disturbed as it took valuable time away from his worship to Allah. Mansur gave him permission to leave and personally saw him out of the palace out of respect. As he saw Imam Ja'far out of the door, his body began to shake and tremble violently. The minister was dumbstruck by everything that happened and asked the Caliph what was going on. Mansur told the minister and servant that at the moment Imam Ja'far walked in the palace a huge deadly snake appeared over my throne. It was moving its tongue viciously making it clear in no uncertain terms not to harm Imam Ja'far otherwise the snake would overthrow his throne which would have meant the end of him. It was for that reason that I behaved in an unaccustomed and unusual way in fear of the snake.

*Tazkiratul al-Awliya*

To trouble or to tease the friends of Allah is a very bad thing, which invites trouble.

• 356 •

# Expensive clothing

Imam Ja'far al-Sadiq☼ once wore very bright and expensive looking clothing. A person remarked, 'O son of the Messenger of Allah! It is unlike of his family to wear such clothes.' He grabbed his hand and placed it inside his sleeve and asked him what he felt. He replied that it felt rough and coarse inside that would make one itch all day long. Imam Ja'far said, 'What you felt inside is for the Creator, and the material you see on the outside is for the created.'

*Tazkiratul al-Awliya*

The friends of Allah on the face of it appear to live normal worldly lives, but their reality is that they are disconnected from the world, and are well and truly linked to Allah's will.

• 357 •

# Moneybag

A person lost his purse. They came across Imam Ja'far al-Sadiq☼ and accused him of taking it. He was oblivious to who he was accusing. Imam

Ja'far did not contest the man and asked him how much loss he had incurred. He replied a thousand dinars. He took him to his house and gave him the said amount and they went their separate ways. The following day the man found his lost purse with the money intact. He returned to Imam Ja'far still not knowing who he was and apologised to him for falsely accusing him and tried his level best to return the thousand dinars but he refused it. He said to him, 'The money is yours. When we give, we don't take it back.' The man went on his way and asked his friend about this person. He was informed it was no other than Imam Ja'far al-Sadiq. On hearing this he hung his head in shame for his actions and for ignorance as to who this generous being was.

*Tazkiratul al-Awliya*

---

The Friends of Allah have no desire or aspirations for this world. To them material goods is like a 'necessary evil'. For them Allah and His Prophet ﷺ are enough.

• 358 •

# Harun al-Rashid and a Bedouin

Caliph Harun al-Rashid once came to the *Haram Sharif* in Makkah and ordered that the *Haram Sharif* be cleared so that he could perform Tawaf. The *mataaf* was cleared and he began the ritual when out of nowhere a Bedouin like figure with his face veiled came and began the Tawaf. Harun did not like this at all and looked towards his servant. The servant then went to stop the stranger from going round the Ka'bah. "O Bedouin! Don't you know that the Caliph wants to do Tawaf?" But the stranger replied, "Here at Allah's House all people small or big, young or old rich or poor are all the same. Who is big and who is small I don't know. Go away and do not disturb me." Harun heard this comment and told his servant to leave him alone.

After doing Tawaf, Harun went towards the al-Hajr al-Aswad, but before he reached it the Bedouin came and quickly kissed it. Harun then went to Maqam Ibrahim but the Bedouin again reached there before the Caliph. After completing the rites, Harun ordered his servant to call the Bedouin over. The servant went and conveyed the Caliph's message to the stranger. The man replied, "I have no desire to meet him. If he wants to meet me he should come and see me." The servant became angry by this comment and went back to Harun. He heard these comments and agreed that he in fact should go and meet him. He stood before the stranger and offered salaam to which the stranger replied. He then sought his permission to sit down. The Bedouin said, "This House is neither yours nor mine, it belongs solely to Allah so how can I grant you permission? Here we are all equal. If you wish then sit down, if not then go back to where you have come from." Harun was impressed by the strange man's eloquence and style and sat down and began to talk.

"Could you give me some knowledge? I would be more than grateful." The stranger replied, "Do you want to know as a teacher or as a pupil?" "As a pupil" replied Harun. "Okay then listen carefully as if you are a pupil." Harun sat as a pupil sits in front of a teacher and began asking questions. The Bedouin replied, "Shall I tell you one thing, or five things or seventeen things. Shall I tell you twenty-four things or ninety-four? From forty shall I tell you one, or should I spend a whole lifetime on just one?" Hearing this Harun laughed by saying that he asked for only one answer. "O Harun! If there is not any limit to religion, then on the Day of Judgement there would be no limit to the number of questions the Creator would ask the created." He then recited the following verse from Sura al-Anbiya. "And We shall set up the scales of justice on the Day of Resurrection - therefore no soul will be wronged in the least; and if a thing is equal to a grain of mustard seed, We will bring it; and We are Sufficient to (take) account." Harun noticed that the man did not call him by proclaiming 'Amirul Momineen'. This made him very angry and threatened to kill him behind Mount Safa and Marwa. But the Servant told Harun that the stranger was protected by virtue of being within the precincts of the *Haram Sharif.* The Bedouin heard this talk and began to laugh and giggle much to the bemusement of the other men. "Why are you laughing?" they asked. He replied "One of you are bringing forward death when it is far off, and the other is staving off death when it has already arrived!" Harun heard this and hung his head in shame. He again pleaded with the stranger to tell him an obligation (Fardh)? The stranger did not let Harun wait any longer and told him his answer. "Allah has made many things Fardh upon me, and you want just one of them which is the religion of Islam. The five Fardh are the five prayers. And in those five prayers there are seventeen Fara'idh. They are the seventeen rakats day and night. (Fajr 2; Zuhr 4; Asr 4; Maghrib 3 and Isha 4) and the twenty-four Fardh? They are the prostrations day and night. And the twenty-four are the Takbeers of the seventeen rakats. And of the forty, one which is Fardh by this I mean Zakat (1/40 = 2.5%). And the Fardh of a lifetime is Hajj." Harun heard the simplicity and beauty of the stranger's words and became attracted towards him. The Bedouin gave the answer to Harun's question and now sought the answer to his question from him? Harun gave him permission to ask. "O Amirul Momineen! What do you say about a man who sees a woman in the morning who is unlawful for him, but at midday she becomes lawful for him. At night she again becomes forbidden upon him, but come the morning she is again lawful and pure. At noon, she is then unlawful but come Asr time she is okay again. At sunset she is again impure for him, but come nightfall he is allowed to have her." Harun heard this and was lost in the words and the meanings and the sequence of events. He pleaded with the stranger to provide the answer to the question himself. "You are a great man with authority over the people. Why can't you answer this simple problem?" Harun said "Allah has indeed blessed you with a rank far higher than me. I ask you for the sake of the *Haram Sharif* we are in to give the answer to this puzzle?" The stranger said. "The women the man saw in the morning was a slave-girl. She was forbidden for him. At Zuhr he brought her making her lawful. At Asr he freed her, making her once again unlawful for him. At sunset he marries her making her completely lawful for him. But at night he divorces her making it illegal again. The next morning he went back on his divorce (legally) thus making her permissible again. At noon he became apostate, making her illegal. But then at Asr he re-entered the fold Islam. At sunset she became an apostate. But at night she accepted Islam again making her lawful once again."

Harun al-Rashid was astounded by the wisdom and knowledge displayed by the Bedouin. He immediately ordered that he be given ten thousand dinars. He flatly refused it saying that he had no need for it. Harun then offered land as a reward for services. But the stranger refused any land offer as well. "My Master if he wishes would grant me a fiefdom. I do not need one."

Harun Al-Rashid returned from the *Haram Sharif* after this strange encounter and began to enquire about him. He eventually learnt that the personality was the son of Imam Ja'far al-Sadiq - Imam Musa Raza who had chosen a lifestyle of Zuhd. Harun al-Rashid heard this and ran back to greet Imam Musa Raza ibn Imam Ja'far al-Sadiq ibn Imam Muhammad ibn Mawla Ali ibn Abu Talib and kissed him on the forehead and treated him with utmost respect.

*Al-Raudhal Al Faiq*

---

The Ahl al-Bayt have great knowledge and wisdom. We also learn that the early rulers and kings of Islam eventually learnt to love and gain knowledge from the wise elders.

# PART SEVEN

## THE FOUR IMAMS OF FIQH

## (MAY ALLAH BE PLEASED WITH THEM ALL)

يَوْمَ نَدْعُواْ كُلَّ أُنَاسٍ بِإِمَـٰمِهِمْ ۖ فَمَنْ أُوتِىَ كِتَـٰبَهُۥ بِيَمِينِهِۦ
فَأُوْلَـٰٓئِكَ يَقْرَءُونَ كِتَـٰبَهُمْ وَلَا يُظْلَمُونَ فَتِيلًا

The day when We shall call every people with their leaders, then
whosoever is given his record in his right hand, they shall read their
records and their rights shall not be suppressed a single thread.

(17:71)

• 359 •

# Imam of the Muslims al-Imam al-A'zam Abu Hanifa﷽

When Imam Abu Hanifa reached the tomb of the Holy Prophet, he said, "Peace be with you, O leader of the Prophets." He immediately heard a reply from the grave saying, "Peace be with you, O leader of the Muslims."

*Tazkiratul al- Awliya*

The Holy Prophet is alive in his grave and responds to greetings made to him. Furthermore we learn that Imam Abu Hanifa is the leader of the Muslims, as referred to by the Holy Prophet.

• 360 •

# The respected old man

Shaykh Ali ibn Uthman al-Hujwiri or Daata Ganj Bakhsh as he is more famously known (may Allah be pleased with him) says that once when he was in Syria he fell asleep near the tomb of Sayyiduna Bilal. In his dream he saw the Holy Prophet enter al-Masjid-al-Haraam carrying an old man in his lap. I ran and kissed the feet of the Holy Prophet and in my heart wanted to ask about the old man, who had been given such an honour. When I got near, the Holy Prophet knew what I would ask and replied, "The leader of the Muslims, Imam Abu Hanifa."

*Kashf al-Mahjub and Tazkiratul al- Awliya*

Imam A'zam Abu Hanifa's⸢ judgements and decisions were in harmony with the Sunnah of the Messenger of Allah⸢. He had his support in every sense of the word.

• 361 •

# The guide

One day Imam Abu Hanifa⸢ was walking along when he saw a boy walking in puddles. The Imam said to the boy, "Be careful that you do not slip and fall over." The boy replied, "O leader of the Muslims, if I fall I will be able to set myself free. It is only I that will be troubled. But what about you! If you put a foot in the wrong direction, then all those following you will be misguided, and at such a point it will be a difficult situation to control." On hearing this remark his eyes were filled with tears.

*Tazkiratul al- Awliya*

Imam Abu Hanifa is the leader of the Muslims. This story tells us of the burden and responsibility an Imam has over his followers. For on the Day of Judgement it is the Imam that will be accountable for his decisions regarding the Muslim Ummah.

• 362 •

# Night vigil Imam

Imam Abu Hanifa⸢ used to read 300 rak'ats (units of worship) of Nafl (voluntary) prayer every night. One day the Imam was walking when he heard a man talking to a friend saying that Imam A'zam reads 500 units of Nafl each night. On hearing this the Imam made the intention that from now on he would read 500 units of extra prayer each night, so that what was said of him was true.

Once the Imam was with a few of his close students, when one of them said, "Did you know that people say that our Imam spends the whole night in the remembrance of Allah, and does not sleep a wink"? The Imam heard this and said, "From now on this is exactly what I will do." The reason for the Imam to make such a decision was that Allah says that whoever hears of praise about himself, which he likes, but does not have that particular quality in them and does not act upon it then they will never escape the punishment of Allah. Hence, from then on the Imam spent all night in worship. In actual fact, the ablution that he performed for the late night prayer (Isha), was the same for the Dawn Prayer (Fajr). It is said that he recited the Holy Qur'an 7000 times at the place where he is now buried.

*Tazkiratul al- Awliya & Jawahir ul Bayan fi Tarjama al-Khayrat al-Hisaan*

---

Our Imam was a person that was awake in the night, engaged in praise and worship of his Lord, which is why the Almighty blessed him with such a high status in the Ummah.

• 363 •

# Fatwa and Taqwa

One day Imam A'zam Abu Hanifa﷽ was walking through the market when some dirt the equivalent of a nail came on his clothes. He went straight to the riverbank and started to wash it off. The people saw this and said "O Imam! You tell us that if dirt of this amount comes on to our clothes it is permissible to pray but yet you are scrubbing your clothes?" Imam A'zam﷽ said, "What you have said is true. But that was my Fatwa and this is my Taqwa."

*Tazkiratul al- Awliya*

---

Imam A'zam﷽ epitomised *taqwa* in all his actions. Have we ever stopped to think of ourselves and if our clothes are clean enough to pray to Allah?

• 364 •

# Chief Judge

The Caliph Mansoor offered Imam Abu Hanifa﷽ the job of chief judge. The Imam turned down the offer and said that he was not worthy of the title. This did not impress him and he called the Imam a liar and said, "That there is nobody more worthy of this title than you." The Imam replied, "If I am a liar than obviously I cannot be the chief justice." Imam Abu Hanifa﷽ got up and left.

*Tazkiratul al- Awliya*

---

Those who are close to Allah have no value for worldly titles and honours. So what right do those people who pursue worldly desires have in criticising the likes of Imam Abu Hanifa who are distant from the world and its pleasures?

# Perfection of piety

One day Imam Abu Hanifa was on his way to lead a funeral prayer. It was a very hot day and the sun was beating down, and there was no shelter to stay cool. Nearby there was a house where one could get shelter. The people asked the Imam to stand against the house but the Imam said, "The house owner owes me some money, if I start using his house as a shelter then it may look as though I am taking interest for the money I have lent him. As our Holy Prophet has said that anyone taking profit on the money that they lend is considered as being interest. I do not want to be amongst those who take interest." Therefore he remained in the baking heat.

*Tazkiratul al- Awliya*

Imam Abu Hanifa is without doubt amongst the God fearing. The constant reference to the sayings of the Prophet of Allah illustrate that all decisions were weighed against the laws of Islam.

# Impact of Qur'an recitation

Yazid ibn Layth who is considered amongst the righteous people narrates the following story. "One day, we performed Isha prayer in which the Imam recited Sura al-Zalzalah (The Earthquake). Imam Abu Hanifa was following the prayer. After the congregation finished he was sitting in a reflective mood and was taking cold deep breathes. I got up from there and went away and left the lantern on as Imam A'zam was still sitting there. There was a little oil left in that lantern. When I returned in the early morning for Fajr, I saw Abu Hanifa as I left him in a reflective mood. Imam Abu Hanifa was holding his head and was saying to himself, "O You who will reward the good even of the weight of an atom and who will punish even the weight of an atom, save Nu'man (Abu Hanifa's first name) with your Grace on the Day of Reckoning from the Hell fire and do not let him go near it. And welcome him in your countless mercies." When I entered, Imam Abu Hanifa saw me and said, "Do you want the lantern?" I said, "I have come to recite the Fajr Azan. He then said to me, "What you just saw, do not tell anyone, keep it secret."

**When the earth is shaken as, its shaking is appointed.**

**And the earth throws out its burden.**

**And man says, 'what happened to her'?**

**That day it shall narrate all its news.**

**For your Lord has sent command to her.**

**On that day, people will return towards their Lord being in different ways, so that they may be shown their deeds.**

**Then whosoever has done good of a weight of an atom shall see it.**

**And whosoever has done evil of a weight of an atom shall see it.**

*Jawahirul Bayaan fi tarjuma Al-Khayraat ul Hisaan*

---

Imam Abu Hanifa was not only a great and accomplished Imam but also a very pious god-fearing person and a gnostic (Arif) of Allah. We learn the extent of his reflections on each verse and Surah of the Qur'an. So how can it be then when it came to the issues and fatwas of Shariah and worship, he was wrong or misled? Those people who criticise him are misled themselves.

• 367 •

## Fear of Judgement Day

Imam Abu Hanifa ﷺ was walking along when unknowingly he trod on a boy's foot. The boy said, "O Shaykh! Don't you fear the retribution of the Day of Judgement?" Imam heard this and fainted. When he regained consciousness he thought of these words as a warning and instruction.

*Jawahirul Bayaan*

---

Imam Abu Hanifa ﷺ despite being a great scholar and leader had an immense amount of fear of the Day of Judgement. Indeed the people of knowledge are more fearful of this day even though they are guided and saved. So what can be said about us ignorant and lazy people who neglect our Islamic duties and are not fearful of the Day when we will be held accountable for all our deeds?

• 368 •

## The cobbler

There lived in Imam Abu Hanifa's ﷺ neighbourhood a cobbler. He was a very bright and colourful character. It was his routine to labour all day and then to spend the night eating and drinking with his friends. Imam A'zam ﷺ due to his own routine of worship during the night would sleep little. He would sometimes overhear his neighbour's frolics and sometime ignore it. One night the cobbler was out enjoying himself when he was arrested.

The following morning, Imam A'zam ﷺ enquired from his followers about the cobbler because he did not hear any noise that night. His followers found out that he had been arrested and was in jail. Imam A'zam Abu Hanifa ﷺ immediately wore his cloak and called for a vehicle to take him to the Governor's house.

They learnt that Imam A'zam was on his way and duly made preparations for his arrival. The Governor personally received Imam Abu Hanifa as he got there. After greeting him the Governor said to Imam A'zam, "O Imam! Why the trouble? We would have come to see you." Imam A'zam went on to tell the Governor that in his neighbourhood was a cobbler who had been arrested by the chief police officer. It was his wish that he be released. The Governor sent an order to release the man. Imam A'zam then left the Governor and accompanied the cobbler back home. Imam A'zam said to the cobbler, "We have not let you go to waste." The cobbler replied, "You have honoured the right of a true neighbour." The cobbler was so touched by the Imam's gesture that he renounced his lavish lifestyle and chose a life in the company of his respected neighbour. The cobbler went on to attain a great status as a jurist in his own right.

*Haywatul Haiwan*

---

Imam A'zam ﷺ was not only a great scholar and jurist but also a great neighbour. We learn from this story that it is our religious and moral duty to look out for our neighbours whether they are good people or bad. Imam A'zam's attention towards this person turned him into a great servant of Islam.

**• 369 •**

# Kindness and generosity

Shafeeq says that they were walking along with Imam A'zam Abu Hanifa🙵 when a person saw them and suddenly changed direction into a side street. Imam A'zam saw him and called him over. Imam A'zam asked the person why he changed direction. The person replied, "O Imam! I am indebted to you. I owe you ten thousand dinars. This debt has been on me for some while now. I am really tight for money and I am really ashamed." Imam A'zam said, "All praise to Allah! Because of me you have such a state of mind. Go! For I have forgiven the debt and I give witness to that. From now on you do not need to hide from me and for that fear you had in your heart for me, please forgive me."

*Jawahir ul Bayaan*

Imam A'zam🙵 was a very kind and generous being. He forgave the person willingly on seeing his state of mind. We too should follow the footsteps of Imam A'zam and all the friends of Allah by willing to forgive and forget. We should also strive for the hereafter rather than the wealth of this mortal world.

**• 370 •**

# Imam's insight

Some boys were playing with a ball when the ball landed in the middle of a gathering in which Imam A'zam Abu Hanifa🙵 was present. No boy had the courage or audacity to go into the gathering and fetch the ball. One boy said to the others, "If you ask me I will go and get it." The boy then went inside the gathering and fetched the ball. Imam A'zam﷽ saw this and said, "It seems that this boy is not legitimate." The people in the gathering asked about the boy and found out that the boy was an illegitimate child. The people asked "Imam! How did you know?" Imam A'zam replied, "If he was legitimate he would have shame which would have prevented him from doing what he did."

Tazkiratul al- Awliya

---

To have utmost respect and shame for elders is a sign of goodness and nobility.

• 371 •

# Silencing response

An opponent of Imam A'zam Abu Hanifa﷽ approached him said, "What is your fatwa (legal decision) on such a person who doesn't yearn for Paradise and doesn't fear the Hell or Allah? This person eats dead meat and offers prayer without Ruku or Sajda. He gives testimony without seeing. He doesn't like the truth and keeps Fitna (trials and tribulations) as his friends. He flees from mercy and affirms what the Jews and Christians say?"

Imam A'zam looked at one of his followers and asked him what he thought about such a person? The follower replied, "This person appears to be very bad and has the characteristics of disbelief (kufr)." Imam A'zam smiled and said, "No! In actual fact such a person is a friend of Allah and is a complete and true believer." Imam A'zam﷽ then looked and said, "If I give you a response to your question, will you stop saying ill about me?" The person agreed as Imam A'zam went on to explain. "This person does not seek Paradise but Allah alone and does not fear Hell but Allah alone. Moreover he is content with the promise of Allah. The dead animal he eats is fish. And the prayer he offers without Ruku and Sajda is Salutations upon Sayyiduna Muhammad ﷺ. Giving testimony without seeing is his belief in Allah. He doesn't like death, which is true because it will shorten his lifespan in which to worship Allah. Wealth and children is fitna that he has kept with him. The mercy he flees from is when it rains. And he testifies what the Jews and Christians do. "And the Jews spoke, "The Christians are nothing," and Christians spoke; "The Jews are nothing," though they read the Book.... (2:113) The person heard this silencing response stood up and kissed Imam A'zam ﷺ on the forehead and swore that he spoke the truth.

*Jawahir ul Bayan fi tarjamaatul al Khayratul Hisaan*

---

Imam A'zam ﷺ is such a blessing and gift to the Ummah that he solved with ease any problems that were presented to him. His decisions were always within the framework of Qur'an and Sunnah.

• 372 •

# Deceit

The enemies of Imam A'zam Abu Hanifa ﷺ hatched a scheme to blacken his name and reputation. They hired a woman who went to Imam A'zam ﷺ and said that her husband was ill and wanted him to come and pray over him so he could get better. Imam A'zam went with the lady to her house. When he got there, the lady locked the doors to the rooms and started to scream and shout. The enemies of Imam A'zam leading this plot came to the scene and took the lady and Imam A'zam away to the Caliph to report the matter. The

Caliph jailed the pair, as their case would be decided in the morning. Imam Abu Hanifa⊛ spent the whole night in prayer (as he usually would). The lady saw him worship Allah Almighty and felt mightily ashamed of framing such a pious and God-fearing person. She fell at the feet of Imam A'zam⊛ and explained the whole plot. Imam A'zam accepted her forgiveness and asked her to do one thing. He asked her to make some excuse to the jail guards of leaving the cell. Once she did that, he asked her to go to his house and tell his wife Umme Hammad what was happening. The lady managed to be excused from the jail and went straight to Imam A'zam's house. She woke up Umme Hammad and explained to her the whole story. Umme Hammad went and took the place of the lady in the prison cell.

Morning came and the enemies of Imam Abu Hanifa all turned up hoping to see his great name and reputation being tarnished. On the orders of the Caliph, the lady and Abu Hanifa were called forward to explain themselves. The Caliph said, "O Abu Hanifa! Do you believe it is acceptable to be alone with a strange woman?" Imam A'zam replied, "With whom?" The Caliph said, "The woman in front of you." Imam Abu Hanifa then called his mother-in-law forward as a witness to identify the lady in question. Imam A'zam said to her, "Can you lift the veil of this woman and tell the court who this lady is?" The lady did as she was told and saw her daughter sitting there. "O Caliph! This is my daughter, Umme Hammad. She is married to Imam Abu Hanifa. What is all the fuss about?" The enemies heard this and were humiliated as the case was thrown out of the Caliph's court. Imam A'zam's name and reputation remained intact.

*Nuzahatul Majaalis*

---

Imam Abu Hanifa⊛ had many enemies and opponents in his lifetime and the same is true 1300 years later. But the enemies of the friends of Allah were defeated then and they will be defeated and humiliated now.

# Imam Abu Hanifa and Imam Malik

One day Imam A'zam Abu Hanifa attended a lesson (dars) given by Imam Malik. Imam Malik did not recognise Imam A'zam at the time. He was presenting an issue that Imam A'zam disagreed on. He spoke out and gave his own opinion on the issue. Imam Malik enquired as to where this gentleman had come from? He said, "I come from Iraq." Imam Malik replied, "What the land of trials and tribulations"? Imam A'zam said, "Can I recite to you a verse from the Holy Qur'an?" He said, "Go ahead." Imam A'zam read the following verse: "And some villagers around you are hypocrites and some of the people of Iraq too. Hypocrisy has become their habit"...

Imam A'zam deliberately read "people of Iraq" instead of "people of al-Madina" as it should be. His aim was to testify what Imam Malik had just read. Imam Malik said, "The ayat should read "people of al-Madina" not "people of Iraq." Imam A'zam said, "Thanks to Allah that you attribute yourself what you labelled on me." Imam A'zam got up and left the gathering. When Imam Malik found out who he was he called him over and greeted him and treated him with great honour and respect.

*Nuzahatul Majaalis*

---

Imam A'zam Abu Hanifa had a great ability to give instant responses in the light of Qur'an and Hadith. His scholastic abilities were recognised by other great Imams of that time.

# Change of brides

A man got his two daughters married off to another person's two sons. The Walima was arranged for the following day in which the great Imam🙷 also attended. The father of the two brides came out of his house in a state of panic. The night before, the brides got mixed up and went in the wrong bedrooms. When morning came they realised what had happened. Sufyaan, a scholar also present, said that there was no blame as it was an accident and suggested that the right couple's stay with each other. Imam A'zam kept quiet on the issue. Imam A'zam was then approached and was asked for his opinion. Imam A'zam requested for the two grooms to be called over. The grooms presented themselves to Imam A'zam who asked them, "Did you like the woman you spent the night with?" Both grooms said that they did. Imam A'zam suggested that since this was the case, they should divorce their original wives and marry the other. The grooms divorced their original wives and because the marriage was not consummated, the Iddat period was not compulsory. So what happened was that they re-married that day.

*Jawahir ul Bayaan*

---

Imam A'zam🙷 demonstrated his wisdom and foresight in dealing with this complicated case. Imam A'zam by the blessings of his comprehensive command of the Qur'an and Hadith and his practice of the deen helped him deal with similar and equally difficult issues throughout his life.

# Hole in the wall

Judge Ibn Abi Ya'la had a case in his court where a person came and requested to make a window in his wall. But his neighbour was opposing the planning permission. The judge called the neighbour and asked him why he was opposing the window. The person gave his reasons, and the judge ruled in his favour. Imam A'zam ﷺ found out about the decision and approached the person and said to him to request from the judge permission to knock the wall down completely. The person put forward this request to the judge, as it was every house owner's right to knock his wall down. The judge had no option but to give permission to knock the wall down. The successful applicant announced that his wall was being knocked down. The neighbour became very anxious and went to the judge and requested that he allowed the construction of the window in the wall and to prevent the whole wall coming down. The judge understood the briefing the neighbour received from Imam Abu Hanifa ﷺ and gave permission to put a window in the wall.

*Jawahir ul Bayaan*

Imam Abu Hanifa ﷺ demonstrated his quick thinking and comprehensive knowledge of the law by instructing the person in getting his wish fulfilled by the judge. His suggestions were always full of wisdom.

# Counsel and wisdom

A young neighbour of Imam Abu Hanifa approached him about a problem he had. He wished to marry a girl but the family of the girl were asking for a dowry more than he could afford. Imam Abu Hanifa ordered him to do Istikhara (a prayer to Allah asking for guidance). After doing so he got permission to marry. The family of the bride would not allow their daughter to leave until the boy had offered the dowry. Imam A'zam told the boy to get a loan. The boy paid it and took his bride home. The next day Imam A'zam instructed the boy to go to his in-laws and inform them that he intended to live with his wife somewhere far away. The in-laws heard this and became very anxious. They went to Imam A'zam and complained and sought his fatwa on the issue. Imam Abu Hanifa replied, "The young husband has a right to take his new wife wherever and whenever he wants." The in-laws replied, "But we cannot possibly cope without seeing our daughter live nearby." Imam A'zam told the in-laws to give back whatever they took from him and make him happy so that he stays and does not move elsewhere. The in-laws agreed on the condition that the boy did not try to leave. Imam A'zam told the young man about the agreement however he tried to make the most of the opportunity and said, "I want more than this." Imam A'zam said, "Do you accept the fact that while you owe money to people you try and live elsewhere?" The young man said, "For God's sake! Do not mention this to anyone otherwise I will get nothing."

*Jawahirul Bayaan*

Imam Abu Hanifa was an extremely ingenious and wise scholar and Imam. The decision made above illustrates this fact clearly. We also learn that in laws should not impose dowry on grooms that are out of their ability, otherwise it leads to problems.

# Lost treasure

A person buried some of his valuable possessions in the ground and forgot where he had buried it. He tried his best to remember but could not. He approached Imam Abu Hanifa ﷺ and asked his advice. He ﷺ told the man to go and spend the whole night in prayer. By doing so, he will remember where his lost treasure was. The man went away and did as he was told. The man had prayed only a few rak'ats when he remembered where his treasure was. He became very happy and the next morning went to tell Imam A'zam ﷺ about the good news and said to him, "Imam! What wonderful advice you gave me, I have found my wealth." Imam A'zam replied, "I knew Shaytan the accursed would not let you pray all night, that's why he prompted you about the wealth. What a shame you did not spend the rest of the night in true gratitude to Allah Almighty for finding your lost treasure."

*Jawahir ul Bayan*

When people face difficulties and problems they are quick to remember Allah and seek His help. But when the difficulties go away, they are also quick in forgetting to be grateful to Allah. Such behaviour is not characteristic of true Muslims. A true Muslim is one who is remembering Allah Almighty in all states whether he is healthy or ill, rich or poor.

# Son-in-law

There was a person in the time of Imam Abu Hanifa who showed disrespect and contempt for the third rightly guided caliph Sayyiduna Uthman and called him a Jew (Allah forbid!). Imam A'zam found out about this person and called him over. Imam A'zam told this man that he had found the ideal match for his daughter to marry. Imam A'zam told him that he had every good quality a person could wish in a husband. But the only thing about him was that he was a Jew. The man said to Imam A'zam, "What a shame that such a great scholar and jurist like you think that it is appropriate to marry a Muslim daughter with a Jew. I will not let such a marriage to take place." Imam A'zam said, "What does your opinion count for when the Prophet of Allah deems it appropriate to marry not one but two of his daughters to a person you call a Jew?" The person realised the valuable point Imam A'zam was trying to make and immediately apologised for his wrong beliefs and decided to keep company with Imam A'zam and gain from his knowledge and wisdom.

*Tazkiratul al- Awliya*

---

Imam Abu Hanifa was a great Imam and guide for the Muslims. He explained the true Aqidah in such a way that people who previously had hatred for great and noble characters soon became true believers. We also learn that contempt and disrespect for Sayyiduna Uthman is in reality contempt for the Prophet of Allah and whosoever has contempt for him, there is no help.

# Husband and wife

A husband and wife had a misunderstanding between each other, which led to the husband in anger saying to his wife that he will not speak to her until she spoke to him first. The wife too took a vow and said that she would not speak to him unless he spoke first. With no one talking to each other, the house had become a living nightmare. After a few very difficult days of living with his wife, the husband went to Imam A'zam﷽ and explained the situation. Imam Abu Hanifa﷽ said to the husband to go to his wife and call her happily, you would not be blamed for doing so. This is because when you said I would not talk to you unless you speak first but if she does not respond then you will be at fault. But she said, "I swear to God I will not talk to you until you talk to me." So after this oath she spoke to you, hence you can speak to her without being at fault.

*Jawahir ul Bayaan*

Imam A'zam's﷽ thinking and analytical approach is so comprehensive that his decisions were better and wiser than those of his contemporaries.

• 380 •

# Identity parade

A burglar entered the house of a person at night and disturbed the owner.

The burglar was aware that the house owner was awake and thought of a way of subduing him. The burglar got hold of the house owner by the throat and threatened him. He said to him that if he revealed his identity then he would divorce his wife three times. The house owner had no choice but to submit to the burglar's conditions and swore an oath of divorcing his wife if he revealed the burglar's identity. The burglar took what he wanted and left the burgled man with a big problem.

Morning came and the burglary became known to the people but the victim could not say anything. He could take no more and went to Imam A'zam﷽ and explained the problem. "O Imam! I know who the burglar is, but I cannot say anything otherwise I will have to divorce my wife." Imam A'zam called upon all the respectable people of the city for advice and decided upon an identity parade. What Imam A'zam said to the man was to see one by one all the suspects and to say "no" to that person who did not burgle his house. And when it came to the burglar he should remain quiet. By doing so he would identify the burglar and keep his oath intact. The man liked the idea and went ahead with it. The identity parade took place and the man said no to each and every suspect who did not burgle his house. And when it came to the turn of the person who did commit the crime the man kept quiet. The man was identified and duly arrested and the victim wriggled his way out of a tricky situation.

*Lata'if ilmiya kitaab al Azkiya*

---

Imam Abu Hanifa﷽ had excellent and comprehensive knowledge of religious and worldly issues, and dealt with awkward situations like this with ease.

# He who digs a hole for others often falls into it

Rabi was the doorkeeper of the palace of Caliph Mansur and held great enmity towards Imam Abu Hanifa. He was a great enemy of Imam A'zam﷽. One day the Caliph invited Imam A'zam who accepted. Rabi said to the Caliph, "O leader of the Muslims! Abu Hanifa says bad things about your forefather Ibn Abbas﷽ and opposes him. Ibn Abbas﷽ said that the person who takes an oath over an issue and after one or two days says "Allah willing" (Insha Allah) that oath does not stand. And Imam A'zam says that the oath taken with the words "Allah willing" will be effective. It will not be reliable afterwards." Imam A'zam﷽ spoke and said, "O leader of the Muslims! Rabi wishes that your army is free from the burden of taking your oath." The Caliph asked, "How is that?" Imam A'zam﷽ continued, "The people will take an oath of support in front of you, but will go home and say, "Allah willing." These people will be free from the obligation." The Caliph Mansur laughed and said "O Rabi! Do not try and tease Imam Abu Hanifa﷽. When Imam A'zam left Mansur's presence, Rabi said to him, "You tried to get me killed today." Imam A'zam replied, "You started it."

*Lata'if Ilmiya Kitaab Al Azkiya, Al Khayraat ul Hisaan*

---

Imam A'zam﷽ had many opponents who were jealous of his knowledge, honour and prestige. They were foolish enough to try and trap him by presenting issues in front of the Caliph. But Rabi ended up only digging a hole for himself and fell right into it. This is the fate of all people who show hatred and contempt for the friends of Allah. The friends of Allah are never defeated and the plotters against them always fall flat faced into the hole they dig themselves.

・ 382 ・

# Tusi's reply

Imam A'zam﷯ enjoyed an extraordinary amount of honour and respect in Abu Ja'far Mansur's court. This caused a lot of resentment and jealously among the high-ranking officials of the court. One day Abul Abbas Tusi asked Imam A'zam a question in Mansur's court. He asked, "O Abu Hanifa! Tell me, if the leader ordered one of us to slay the head of a certain person and its blame and crime is not known to us, in such a situation is it allowed to carry out the order?" Imam Abu Hanifa﷯ said, "Tell me, does the Amir of the Muslims give right or wrong orders?" Tusi replied, "Why would the Amir give wrong orders?" Imam said, "So act upon the order that is given." Tusi was left speechless.

*Al Khayrat ul Hasaan*

---

The people who are envious of the friends of Allah wish somehow that their honour and status is tarnished and lowered. But nothing happens to the friends of Allah like Imam Abu Hanifa﷯. In fact their status and honour and respect in the eyes of the true believers increases. Imam A'zam had many envious opponents, but they were unsuccessful in lowering his true rank and honour. And today we find so called Muslims trying to defame his name and legacy, but their schemes will soon turn to dust.

• 383 •

# Peacock thief

A neighbour of Imam A'zamﷺ had his peacock stolen. He went to Imam
Abu Hanifa and told him about it. Imam A'zam told him to remain quiet.
Imam A'zam shortly after went to the mosque to lead the prayer. Before the
prayer started Imam A'zam turned round and said, "Doesn't the person who
stole my neighbour's peacock feel ashamed of themselves that they steal
somebody else's property and then come to the mosque to pray?" The thief
heard these words and hung his head in shame. Imam A'zam pointed out the
thief and told him to return the peacock, which he duly did.

*Al Khayraat Al Hasaan*

Imam A'zamﷺ time and time again demonstrated his ability to exact justice for
people who sought it. His words and actions were full of wisdom.

• 384 •

# Flour

A'mish (May Allah be pleased with him) was a great Muhaddith and
contemporary of Imam A'zamﷺ. One day he had a row with his wife and in
the heat of the moment said to her that if she informed him that the flour in
the house was finished, or if she wrote down that the flour was finished, if
she signalled that it was finished or if she got someone else to tell him that

the flour was finished, then he would divorce her. The wife was dumbstruck by this and did not know what to do. Somebody suggested to her that she should go and see Imam Abu Hanifa ﷺ. She went and explained to him the predicament. Imam A'zam told the lady to get the empty flour bag and tie it to his clothes when he goes to sleep. When he wakes up he will realise what has happened and your marriage will remain intact. The lady went home and did as Imam A'zam suggested. A'mish woke up the next morning with the flour bag tied to his clothes and realised that the flour in the house had finished. A'mish said, "I swear to Allah! This is the work of Imam Abu Hanifa. While he is alive how can we be successful? He uses our women to put our knowledge to shame."

*Juwahirul Bayan fi Tarjama tul Al Khayrat ul Hisaan*

---

The contemporaries of Imam A'zam ﷺ submitted and acknowledged the scholastic brilliance and wisdom of Imam Abu Hanifa ﷺ.

• 385 •

# Bowl of water

A man asked his wife to bring some water for him in a bowl. She went to fetch the water and as she was going to her husband he said to her, "I will not drink this water. And if you drink it I will divorce you. And if you give it to someone else I will divorce you. And if you spill the water then I will still divorce you." The woman was shocked to hear what her husband was saying and was trying to think of a way of using the water in such a way that would not end in divorce. A person told Imam A'zam ﷺ about the bizarre incident. Imam A'zam ﷺ told the person to go and tell the lady to soak some clothes in that water and put it to dry. The conditions of the husband will be met and she will not be at fault.

*Al- Khayrat ul Hisaan*

---

Allah has blessed Imam A'zam Abu Hanifa with such a comprehensive understanding of things that he could solve seemingly impossible issues with ease. He solved issues in such a way that great thinkers would have to pause to think.

• 386 •

## Chicken's egg

A person swore that he would never eat eggs again. He also swore that he would eat that thing which his friend would cook for him at his house. The man went to his friend who gave him an egg and was baffled as to what to do with his oath. He went to Imam A'zam who told him to place that very egg underneath a chicken and let it hatch it into a baby chicken. He could then sacrifice it and satisfy both of his oaths.

*Al Khayraat ul Hissan*

---

Imam Abu Hanifa's ingenuity and quick thinking is amply illustrated in this short anecdote.

# Engraved ring

A person came across a ring that had somebody else's name on it. The ring had the name Ata ibn Abdullah written on it. He found it difficult to remove the whole name without damaging it and went to Imam A'zam ﷺ for advice. Imam A'zam told him to make the 'ba' of 'ibn' into a 'meem', and then to remove the dot from 'bin' and place a / underneath it. Change the dot from below to above Abdullah to make it now read 'in dillah.' So the engraved ring now had the words Ata min indillah which means 'a gift from Allah.'

*Al Khayraat ul Hisaan*

---

Imam A'zam ﷺ is without doubt a gift from Allah. Any criticism of him and his legacy is in reality a rejection of Allah's gift to the Ummah of the Prophet ﷺ.

# False propaganda

Imam A'zam ﷺ once went to al-Madina al-Munawarra. There he met the grandson of Saydina Ali ibn Abi Talib, Sayyiduna Muhammad ibn Hasan ﷺ. Sayyiduna Muhammad ibn Hasan ﷺ said to Imam A'zam, "Are you that person who uses his own *Qiyas* (analogy) over the sayings of my great grandfather Prophet Muhammad ﷺ?" Imam A'zam said, "Allah forbid! How can this be? Please sit with me, as it is a matter of honouring you, just as it is with the Imam of Prophetsﷺ." Muhammad ibn Hasan﷜ then proceeded to ask him questions. He asked, "Who is weaker- man or woman?" Imam A'zam responded, "Women are." He then asked, "What portion is a woman entitled to?" Imam A'zam said, "Half of a man's share." Imam A'zam then added, "If I favoured my *Qiyas* then I would have ruled the opposite to what is right. If I went by my opinion I would have said that the man's share is less because he is stronger and the woman's share is more because she is weaker." Muhammad ibn Hasan﷜ then asked, "What is better (Afzal) daily, Prayer or fasting?" Imam Abu Hanifa﷜ replied, "Prayer is better." He then asked, "When a woman leaves the state of menstruation will she offer her missed prayers or fasts? Imam A'zam replied, "She will offer her missed fasts." Imam A'zam then added, "If I gave preference to my own opinion I would have said that she should make up missed prayers not fasts." He then asked him, "Is urine an impurity or semen?" Imam A'zam﷜ replied, "Urine is an impurity." Imam A'zam added, "If I stated my opinion over the Prophet's rulings I would have said that a Ghusl (bath) is needed for when urine came out and not for semen." Muhammad ibn Hasan﷜ kissed Imam Abu Hanifa on the forehead and said, "It seems that wrong things have been said and spread about you. You speak the truth."

*Jawahir ul Bayaan*

---

We learn from this valuable account that those people who spread false propaganda about Imam Abu Hanifa﷜ are totally wrong. Imam Abu Hanifa﷜ never gave preference to his opinion over that already stated in Hadith. All his legal decisions are in harmony with Qur'an and Hadith. The family of the Prophet testify to this fact.

# Bag full of coins

A person on his deathbed gave his friend a bag full of money containing 1000 Dinars. The dying man said to his friend to give what he liked out of it to his son when he grew up. The man passed away. When that boy grew up, the friend of his late father handed him the empty bag in which the 1000 Dinars were kept and "honoured" his promise with his friend. The boy, angered by what his late father's friend did, went to Imam A'zam Abu Hanifa 🙶 and complained. Imam A'zam 🙶 called the man over to explain himself. Imam A'zam said to the man, "Your friend said to you that after I die, when my son grows up, give to him "what you like." And seen as you have preferred the 1000 Dinars for yourself I order you to hand that money over to this young man, otherwise you will have not fulfilled your friends dying wish." The man was stumped by this response and handed the money to the boy.

*Jawahir ul Bayaan*

---

We should not be dishonest in dealing with somebody's property. And we should not take for ourselves what belongs rightfully to the orphans. Such an act is a big sin in Islam. Imam A'zam 🙶 was a very wise person and was the remover of difficulties.

# The Bedouin and the barley

One day Imam A'zam﷽ was going somewhere when he lost his way and was in need of some water. He came across a Bedouin who had a water bottle with him. Imam A'zam﷽ asked for some water and the Bedouin declined. The Bedouin would only offer water for five Dirhams. Imam A'zam brought the water for five Dirhams. Imam A'zam had some crushed barley with him and offered it to the Bedouin and said to him to eat as much as he wanted. The crushed barley was mixed with oiled olives. The Bedouin saw this mouth-watering dish and ate as much as he could and as a result became extremely thirsty. The Bedouin asked for some water from Imam A'zam. He told him that it would cost him five Dirhams. The Bedouin had no choice but to pay for the water to quench his thirst. Imam A'zam﷽ got his money back and the Bedouin drank the water.

*Lata'if Ilmiya Kitaab Al Azkiya*

Imam A'zam﷽ used his God-given talent of wisdom and ingenuity to solve problems.

# Response to a Kharjite

Imam Abu Hanifa﷽ was one of many people arrested during the Kharjite insurrection. Imam A'zam﷽ was brought in front of Zahak, the Kharjite leader and according to Kharjite dogma tried to make him repent for his beliefs. Imam A'zam in response to this attempt to make him repent said, "I repent for all acts of disbelief." The Kharjites heard this and let Imam A'zamﷺ go. But after a while, some commotion was stirred up and Imam A'zam was again brought in front of Zahak to answer allegations labelled on him. Zahak said to Imam A'zam, "I hear that the disbelief you repent from is our beliefs?" The Kharjite's belief was that all decisions should be made in accordance with the Qur'an only. Imam A'zamﷺ knowing their beliefs and knew that they would not let him go easily decided to respond from the Qur'an. Imam A'zam said to Zahak that whatever he asked was suspicion and doubt and that he had no proof of what was being said. Zahak said that he was responding only in response to suspicion and doubt. Imam A'zam then read from the Holy Qur'an "...surely suspicion in some certain cases is a sin..." (49:12). Why then Imam A'zam asked were they holding it to be sin before its perpetration? The Kharjite heard this and said, "You say the truth" and released him.

*Jawahirul Bayaan*

---

Imam Abu Hanifaﷺ was such a complete and masterful scholar that he managed to deal with those people who had excluded themselves from the boundaries of Islam. The Kharjites whose opinions derived from only the Qur'an were defeated by Imam A'zam's comprehensive knowledge and understanding of Allah's word. The people of falsehood troubled Imam A'zam a lot but his knowledge defeated them with his sound *aqidah*.

• 392 •

# The mystery of the apple

Imam Abu Hanifaﷺ was sitting with his Companions in the mosque, when a woman entered. She had in her hand an apple that was half red and half pale in colour. She placed the apple in front of Imam A'zam and kept quiet. Imam A'zam picked the apple and split it in half and gave it back to the woman. The woman took the apple and went away. The people present did not understand what had just happened and asked Imam Abu Hanifaﷺ to explain. Imam A'zamﷺ said, "This woman asked me an issue and I gave her the answer." The people were now even more baffled. Imam A'zam said, "This woman placed the apple in front of me and asked me about menstruation. Her blood sometimes comes red and sometimes pale. She wanted to know if the blood was of menses. I split the apple in half and explained to her that not until the blood is clear like the apple inside is she clean. As long as it is coloured as explained, it is the blood of menses."

*Rauz ul Fa'iq*

---

We learn that Imam A'zam was the Imam of all Muslims, men and women alike. He understood issues pertaining to women as well as men and dealt with them in a manner which both males and females felt comfortable with.

• 393 •

# The Day of Reckoning

Nawfal ibn Hayaanﷺ says that when Imam Abu Hanifaﷺ left this world he saw a dream that it was the Day of Judgement, and the whole of mankind was being accounted for their deeds. He saw that the Messenger of Allahﷺ was standing next to his fountain of Kawthar. Besides the Messenger of Allahﷺ stood pious followers. From these pious followers Nawfal ibn Hayan recognised a distinct personality on the right side of the Prophet. The man had a beautiful appearance, and the hairs of his beard were all white. Seeing the huge gathering around the Prophet ﷺ, Nawfal managed to spot Imam Abu Hanifa ﷦ standing on his left. Nawfal ibn Hayaan greeted the Imam and asked him for a glass of water. But the Imam refused by saying, "Water can only be obtained, after permission has been granted by the Messenger of Allah." The Prophet ﷺ granted permission for the water. Upon receiving the water, Nawfal ibn Hayaan asked about this pious personality who was standing on the right hand side of the Prophet. The Imam replied that this is Ibrahim ﷦, and on the left of the Prophet is Abu Bakr Siddiq ﷦, and after this I kept on asking and the Imam continued to introduce the pious personalities.

Tazkiratul al-Awliya

---

Imam Abu Hanifa ﷦ has been blessed with closeness to the Prophet of Allah ﷺ. His Fiqh is such a complete guide that is in complete accordance with the ahadith of the Prophet ﷺ.

• 394 •

# Imam of the Muslims Imam al-Shafi'i ﷦

Imam al-Shafi'i ﷦ states that when he was young he saw the Holy Prophet ﷺ in a dream. The Messenger of Allah asked, "O young man, who are you?" I replied, "O Prophet of Allah, I am your follower." The Prophet drew close to Imam al-Shafi'i and put his blessed saliva in his mouth and said, "Go, the Lord Almighty will shower His mercy upon you." Sayyiduna Ali ﷦ then appeared and put his ring on his finger.

Tazkiratul al- Awliya

---

Imam of the Muslims, Imam al-Shafi'i ﷦ has a great honour and status. This is due to the blessings of Sayyiduna Muhammad's ﷺ blessed saliva and the ring of Mawla Ali ؓ. This helps explain why he is an accomplished scholar and jurist and Imam of the Muslims.

• 395 •

# The genius child

Imam al-Shafi'i's ؓ blessed mother was from the tribe of Banu Hashim (the respectable tribe of Arabia, to which the Holy Prophet belonged), and was a very pious and respected being. The local people would entrust her with their belongings, and they would be safe under her possession. One day two men appeared and presented a box of valuables for safekeeping and went away. A few days later, one of the men returned and asked for their belongings. The valuables were duly retuned. A few more days passed and the second man arrived and asked for the box. The woman replied that his friend had already collected it. This angered the man who said, "We both gave you our valuables, and asked you to return it to both of us. But you have failed to do this." This made her upset. Imam al-Shafi'i had just returned from school and saw what was happening. He told his mother not to worry and asked the man to come with him. The man could not understand what was happening. The Imam replied, "Your box of valuables is present. Come take me to your partner and the goods will be returned." The man was left astonished to the response of the young child as he went to get his valuables.

*Tazkiratul al-Awliya*

Imam al-Shafi'i ؓ from a very young age showed his intellect and genius abilities. When he grew up to be leader of the Muslims these same qualities shone in his decisions and rulings on *Deen*.

# On the throne of Harun al-Rashid

One night Caliph Harun al-Rashid and his wife had an argument. During the argument Zubeidah, his wife, accidentally said that he would burn in Hell. On hearing this Harun said, "If that is the case that I am to burn in Hell, then at this very point, I divorce you." The two of them separated themselves but as Harun loved Zubeaidah so much, he could not bear the separation. He called upon the scholars and wanted to find a solution to this matter. But they were helpless, and just said that only Allah has the knowledge if Harun is to burn in Hell. From the groups of scholars a young man stood up and said: "If the other respected scholars permit, I can address this problem" The other scholars were furious at this young boy, that how will he find a solution to the problem when the other experienced scholars had failed to find a solution? Harun al-Rashid called the young boy towards him and asked him to present his answer. The young boy said, "Do you need me? Or do I need you?" Harun al-Rashid replied, "I need you." The young man asked Harun to come down from his throne and let him be seated on it. The boy explained that a scholar's rank is higher than a king's. He then asked, "Have you ever stopped yourself from committing a sin even though you have the power to commit it, just for the fear and sake of Allah?" Harun replied, "Yes, I swear by God." The young boy declared that Harun was not of those destined for the Hell fire. The other scholars were not satisfied with the decision and asked him to give evidence for his decision. The boy read the following verses from the Holy Qur'an:

**"But as to him who feared to stand before his Lord**
**and restrained his self from evil desires.**
**Then undoubtedly the Paradise is his destination"**

(79:40-41)

This satisfied the scholars and they praised the young boy and prayed for his knowledge. The young man in question was no other than Imam al-Shafi'i ﵀.

*Tazkiratul al-Awliya*

---

Imam al-Shafi'i ﵀ was blessed with immense knowledge of Islam. His ability to reach a very high status in the world of knowledge and jurisprudence is reflected in the story above. The position and status of Imam is like that of an emperor or king but better.

• 397 •

# The Priests

The Christian Emperor of Rome would send gifts every year to Harun al-Rashid. One year he sent his priests to go and challenge Harun al-Rashid about his faith. The Emperor told his priests that if they lost the debate with the Islamic scholars then he would continue sending gifts. On hearing this, Harun al-Rashid called upon his scholars of Islam and took them to the banks of the river and invited the Christian priests there as well. Imam al-Shafi'i ﵀ was also present. Harun al-Rashid pleaded to Imam al-Shafi'i ﵀ to conduct this debate on behalf of the Muslims. Imam al-Shafi'i accepted the invitation and rolled out his prayer mat on the river and sat on it. Neither he sank nor any water come in through the prayer mat. Then the Imam ordered anyone who wished to challenge him, to come and do the same so they could debate. When the Christian priests saw this miracle they all entered the fold of Islam. When the Emperor of Rome heard about this, he was saddened and said, "Thank God the Imam did not perform this miracle in Rome otherwise the whole empire would have accepted Islam."

Tazkiratul al Awliya

---

The friends of Allah have a distinct rank. Their blessings and miracles are such that people embrace Islam immediately on seeing them.

• 398 •

# Insight

Imam al-Shafi'i and Imam Ahmad ibn Hanbal (may Allah be pleased with them both), were sitting in the mosque when a man appeared and started praying. The two Imams looked at him as Imam Ahmad said that this man is an ironmonger. Imam al-Shafi'i disagreed and said that he was a woodcutter. The man finished his prayer, and they asked him what job he did? The man replied that, he previously used to work in ironmongery, but was now a woodcutter.

Nuzhatul Majalis

---

The friends of Allah speak only true words. What they utter is not idle talk. This confirms their nobility and knowledge, wisdom and foresight.

# The heirs of the Prophets

Rabi saw in a dream that Adam had left this world and the people were lifting his coffin for the funeral. He was deeply moved by the dream, and went to see an interpreter to see what it meant. The interpreter of the dream replied, "Your dream tells me that a very great scholar of Islam will die soon. This is because Allah says in the Qur'an that He taught him all the names." Adam is the epitome of knowledge. A few days went by and people heard the news that Imam al-Shafi'i had departed from this world.

*Tazkiratul al-Awliya*

The Imams of the religion are the heirs of the Prophets of Allah (peace be upon them). The Imams of the religion derive benefits from the Prophets. Imam al Shafi'i is without doubt a great scholar of this Ummah as his life and death has been attributed with Adam the father of mankind and Allah's first Prophet.

# Imam of the Muslims Imam Ahmad ibn Hanbal

Baghdad at one time was in the stranglehold of the Mu'tazila. They tried to pressurise Imam Ahmad ibn Hanbal to say that the Holy Qur'an is part of creation (Ma'azallah- Allah forbid!). They tried several ways of getting him to agree with their heretical beliefs. They once invited him to the court where they would debate. At the door of the court stood a man who stopped Imam Ahmad☙ and gave him the following advice. "O leader of the Muslims! Don't ever say that the Holy Qur'an is creation. Remain deaf to their pleas and tricks. This is because once I was accused of theft. They tried to prove I did it and pressurised me into admitting it but I did not accept because I was innocent. In the end I was released. I remained patient in the face of adversity and I have not been blessed like you. You are knowledgeable of the truth therefore remain patient and persistent in your beliefs and stick by them." Imam Ahmad☙ heard these words of advice and was very grateful and felt inspired by them. He said to the doorkeeper, "Thank you very much, May Allah reward you. I will not leave the truth as you advise me to." Imam Ahmad☙ entered the court and began debating with the Mu'tazilas. They attempted to force him to concede that the Qur'an is part of creation. But Imam Ahmad for one moment did not stop in saying the truth about the Holy Qur'an. He was whipped and lashed a thousand times but yet every time he said that the Qur'an is not part of creation. He was in this state of torture that the belt round his trousers came loose. Imam Ahmad whose hands were chained miraculously tied his belt up to conceal his private parts. The people saw this miracle and released him.

*Tazkiratul al-Awliya*

---

Imam Ahmad ibn Hanbal☙ is the Imam of the Muslims. He was a champion and defender of the truth of Islam. He enemies tested him severely but Imam Ahmad☙ remained patient and never ever denied the Truth. For the sake and honour of the Holy Qur'an he put his own life at risk and at the same time protected the Aqidah and Iman of millions of his followers by expressing quite firmly that the Holy Qur'an is Allah's speech and is not a part of creation. We learn that the Imams had immense respect for the Holy Qur'an and ahadith of the Prophet☙ and used them to formulate their *Madhab*, which millions of Muslims follow today.

# Respect and its reward

Imam Ahmad ibn Hanbal۞ was once performing wudu at the riverbank. Another person was also performing wudu further up the riverbank. When that man saw Imam Ahmad۞ he stopped performing wudu, passed Imam Ahmad and resumed his wudu further down the riverbank in respect of Imam Ahmad۞. When that person passed away, someone saw him in their dream and asked that person how Allah Almighty had treated him? The man told the person that when out of respect of Imam Ahmad I went further down the riverbank and performed my wudu, Allah liked this act of respect and honour so much that He has showered His mercies upon me and has granted me salvation.

*Tazkiratul al-Awliya*

Respecting the friends of Allah is a guaranteed way of attaining Allah's eternal happiness. We should therefore love, respect and follow the friends of Allah and seek refuge from those who only show animosity and hatred towards them. Moreover we should avoid the company of such vile people.

# Leavened bread

One day the servant of Imam Ahmad۞ brought some yeast from the judge and made some leavened bread for Imam Ahmad۞. When the bread was presented to Imam Ahmad☙ he asked why the bread was leavened. The servant replied that he had brought some yeast from his son's supplies which is why it was leavened. Imam Ahmad☙ said, "He is the Judge of Isfahan, I cannot eat this and is of no use to me." He then suggested to the servant that if a petitioner came to him he should offer the bread and say, "The yeast is from the judge of Isfahan and the flour is from Imam Ahmad☙, if you wish to eat it have it?"

*Tazkiratul al-Awliya*

---

The people of Allah are extremely fearful and consciousness of Allah. They do not go near those things that are remotely doubtful. So what can be said about us who happily indulge in unacceptable things?

• 403 •

# Knowledge and practice

A student of Imam Ahmad ibn Hanbal☙ came to his house and stayed the night. Imam Ahmad left a jug of water outside his guest's room. When morning came, the water was left as it was. Imam Ahmad asked his student why the water was not used. The student replied, "I had wudu so I worshipped Allah all night otherwise what is the point of seeking knowledge?"

*Tazkiratul al-Awliya*

---

After we seek knowledge we should strive to put that knowledge into practice, otherwise the point of education is defeated. We learn that Muslims of earlier times had immense respect and honour for their teachers.

# Mountains of gold

Imam Ahmad﷽ was passing through some wasteland when he got lost. In search for help he came across a person sitting by himself in the middle of nowhere. Imam Ahmad approached him to ask the way. The person saw Imam Ahmad﷽ and started to cry. Imam Ahmad thought he was hungry and offered him some bread. The man saw the bread and became angry and said, "O Ahmad ibn Hanbal! Who are you to get in between Allah and me? Are you not satisfied with your Lord that you lose your way?" Imam Ahmad﷽ was deeply moved by these words and started to think in his heart, "O Allah! In wastelands you have kept your friends hidden?" The person then said, "O Ahmad! What do you know? Allah has such friends that if they swear by His Holy name then the whole world would turn into gold. When Imam Ahmad looked around, everything appeared in gold. He then heard a hidden voice that said, "O Ahmad! This is such a friend of ours that for his sake we would turn the heavens and earth upside down."

*Tazkiratul al-Awliya*

---

The Friends of Allah have such a high rank and status that they can read people's hearts and minds. And if they wished, they could make mountains of gold. And for their sake Allah would overturn the heavens and earth. All these friends of Allah have a master and leader who is our dear Prophet Muhammad﷽. So what can be said about his authority and proximity to Allah Almighty?

• 405 •

# Ibn Khuzayma's dream

After the passing away of Imam Ahmad ibn Hanbal, a respected man called Muhammad ibn Khuzayma had a dream in which he saw Imam Ahmad. He saw that Imam Ahmad was going somewhere. Ibn Khuzayma asked Imam Ahmad where he was going. Imam Ahmad replied, "I am going to Dar al-salam (The abode of peace). He then asked him, "How did Allah treat you?" Imam Ahmad replied, "He forgave me and placed on my head a crown of glory and gave me shoes to wear. Allah the Almighty said to me, "O Ahmad! All this honour is for you saying that the Qur'an is not created."

*Tazkiratul al-Awliya*

Imam Ahmad earned Allah's pleasure as a result of his knowledge and practice of the Islamic faith. Allah crowned him with glory.

• 406 •

# Imam of the Muslims Imam Malik

Muhammad ibn Abi Al-Siri Asqalani visited the Prophet of Allah in his dream. He asked the Prophet, "O Messenger of Allah! Instruct me so I can propagate this message to the people." Sayyiduna Muhammad said, "O Asqalani! I have given Malik ibn Anas a treasure that I ask you to distribute. The treasure is the *Muwatta*."

*Rauz ul Faiq*

Imam Malik﷽ is the Imam of the Muslims. He is loved and sought after by our Prophet and Master Muhammadﷺ. The *Muwatta* of Imam Malik﷽ is such a collection of approved and certified ahadith that the Messenger of Allahﷻ himself calls it a treasure that is worthy of distributing.

• 407 •

# Respect for knowledge

Harun al-Rashid was visiting al-Madina al Munawarra when he learnt that Imam Malik﷽ was giving lessons (Dars) of his *Muwatta*. He sent a message to Imam Malik telling him to bring his *Muwatta* to him and to read it to him. Imam Malik told the Caliph's messenger that, "Knowledge doesn't go after anyone, it has to be sought. The student always comes to the teacher." Harun al-Rashid heard this and went to Imam Malik's class. Harun al-Rashid sat on a chair and requested Imam Malik to read the *Muwatta* while he listened. Imam Malik said, "I have always taught with the student reading and me listening, hence you will have to do the same." Harun al-Rashid said, "If that is the case then remove these people from here and I will read in private to you." Imam Malik﷽ said, "When the select stop knowledge from reaching the people, it is no longer beneficial." He heard this and started to read when Imam Malik said, "O Harun! To seek knowledge, respect and dignity is needed. Come off the chair and sit in front of me with dignity and read." Hence he got off the chair and sat respectfully in front of Imam Malik and started to read the *Muwatta*.

*Rauz ul Faiq*

To seek knowledge you need to be humble and willing to respect the teacher and what is being taught. We learn from this account that leaders of the previous generations sought knowledge and had a desire to listen to the sayings of our Master Sayyiduna Muhammadﷺ in the company of the friends of Allah﷽.

# Scorpion sting

Imam Malik was once narrating a saying of the Prophet Muhammad when his face all of a sudden became pale, but despite the pain he continued narrating the Hadith. When Imam Malik completed the narration his followers asked him about his pain and discomfort that was visible on his face. Imam Malik lifted his shirt. A scorpion came out and ran away. Imam Malik said, "The scorpion stung me sixteen times while I was narrating the Hadith but out of due respect and honour of these words I did not flinch once."

*Rauz ul Faiq*

The Imams of our faith had great respect and honour for the Hadith of Sayyiduna Muhammad. The Imams of Fiqh took great care in making their decisions in the light of Qur'an and ahadith. When we listen to the Qur'an and ahadith we should also demonstrate great care and attention to these holy and important words.

• 409 •

# Imam Malik's passing away

Imam of the Muslims Imam al-Shafi'i﷦ says that his aunt had a dream in Makkah in which the greatest scholar of the time had passed away. That very day they heard the sad news that Imam Malik, the Imam of al-Madina had passed away.

From Allah we come and to Him is our return.

*Rauz ul Faiq*

Imam Malik﷦ was the greatest and leading scholar (Alim) of his time. Due to his knowledge and excellence he is amongst the four great Imams (may Allah be pleased with them all).

# قصص الألباب

*"There was certainly in their stories a lesson for thos*

Abul Noor
PUBLICATIONS